C000258652

Advanced Introduction to Critical Global Development

Elgar Advanced Introductions are stimulating and thoughtful introductions to major fields in the social sciences, business and law, expertly written by the world's leading scholars. Designed to be accessible yet rigorous, they offer concise and lucid surveys of the substantive and policy issues associated with discrete subject areas.

The aims of the series are two-fold: to pinpoint essential principles of a particular field, and to offer insights that stimulate critical thinking. By distilling the vast and often technical corpus of information on the subject into a concise and meaningful form, the books serve as accessible introductions for undergraduate and graduate students coming to the subject for the first time. Importantly, they also develop well-informed, nuanced critiques of the field that will challenge and extend the understanding of advanced students, scholars and policy-makers.

For a full list of titles in the series please see the back of the book. This is also available on https://www.elgaronline.com/ and https://www.advancedintros.com/ for Elgar Advanced Introduction in Law.

Advanced Introduction to

Critical Global Development

UMA KOTHARI
Professor of Migration and Postcolonial Studies, Global Development Institute, University of Manchester, UK

ELISE KLEIN
Associate Professor, Crawford School of Public Policy, Australian National University, Canberra, Australia

Elgar Advanced Introductions

Edward Elgar
PUBLISHING

Cheltenham, UK • Northampton, MA, USA

Published by
Edward Elgar Publishing Limited
The Lypiatts
15 Lansdown Road
Cheltenham
Glos GL50 2JA
UK

Edward Elgar Publishing, Inc.
William Pratt House
9 Dewey Court
Northampton
Massachusetts 01060
USA

A catalogue record for this book
is available from the British Library

Library of Congress Control Number: 2023937064

ISBN 978 1 80037 607 6 (cased)
ISBN 978 1 80037 609 0 (paperback)
ISBN 978 1 80037 608 3 (eBook)

Printed and bound in Great Britain by
TJ Books Limited, Padstow, Cornwall

For Jay, Kim and Asrar

To all who fight for a more just world

Contents

Acknowledgements x

1 **Introduction: the development landscape** 1
Meanings of development 2
Our approach: centring critical perspectives 4
Historical perspective: colonial legacies and decoloniality 6
Spatial and temporal demarcations 7
Studying development 8
Scope, structure, and organisation of the book 9

2 **Mainstream development histories and ideas** 13
Colonial genealogies of development: imperialism, empire, and settler colonialism 15
Modernisation, coloniality, and the emergence of post-war development 18
Development as economic growth 19
Human development: capabilities and freedoms 24

3 **Borders, boundaries, and classifications** 27
Bordering the discipline 28
The where of development: spatial demarcations 31
Challenging spatial borders and new geographies of development 33
Classifying and categorising the development industry: actors and agents 36
Western public and popular representations of development 37

Shifting the borders: the rising powers and South–
South cooperation   39

4   **Critically (re)thinking development**   **43**
Postcolonial critiques   44
Feminisms and intersectionality   46
Accumulation through dispossession and expulsion   49
Post-development   51
Indigenous knowledges and ontologies   52
Decolonisation and decoloniality   54
Critical thinking   58

5   **Promises of development: employment, health,
and education**   **59**
Working for development: employment and labour   60
Health and development   67
Education: pedagogy of the oppressed   72
Challenging blueprints   75

6   **Migration and mobilities**   **76**
Studying migration, mobility, and development   78
Migration and development approaches   81
Towards migration, development, and decoloniality   84

7   **Degradation and sustainability**   **88**
Development and degradation   89
Political ecology   95
Degrowth and dealing with capitalism   96
Buen Vivir and Earth rights   98

8   **Towards solidarity, decoloniality, and building
the pluriverse**   **101**
Introduction   101
Towards solidarity and justice   102
Towards decolonising development   106
Reparations and redistribution   108

Towards pluriversality   111

References   114
Index   138

Acknowledgements

We would like to thank the many critical scholars and activists with whom we have collaborated over the years, and who have gone before us, for developing and sharing the ideas reflected in this book. We benefited greatly from discussions with colleagues at two events we convened in Naarm (Melbourne): 'New Geographies of Global Inequalities and Social Justice' (2018) and 'Technologies of Bordering: Creating, Contesting and Resisting Borders' (2019).

Uma would like to thank colleagues at the Global Development Institute at the University of Manchester and in the School of Geography at the University of Melbourne for their intellectual insights and for providing convivial working environments. Special appreciation to Niki Banks, Tanja Bastia, Henning Melber, Diana Mitlin, Tanja Mueller, and Lisa Palmer for their ongoing support and friendship. Elise thanks Jon Altman, Dolly Kikon, Carlos Eduardo Morreo, and her other co-contributors and teachers, many of whom are outside the academy, for their generosity, care, and guidance over the years.

We are grateful to Rory Horner for his invaluable feedback on an earlier version of the manuscript, and to Emma Mawdsley for her helpful comments. Thanks also to our research assistant Africa Bauza Garcia-Arcicollar, and to Jacob Henry who so thoroughly and carefully edited the book. We also thank Tim Edensor for engaging with our ideas so thoughtfully.

We would like to pay our respects to the Wurundjeri and Ngunnawal peoples on whose land this book was envisaged and on which much of it was written. We acknowledge ongoing colonisation in what is called Australia and hope this work provides a contribution to struggles to decolonise here and elsewhere.

1 Introduction: the development landscape

The development landscape has never been static, but in these times of uncertainty and insecurity, we are observing profound shifts in global relations, inequalities, and forms of exclusion. We began writing this book during the COVID-19 pandemic, as unequal access to health care and vaccines became ever more pronounced. At the same time, we witnessed and participated in protests against racism and injustice as part of the Black Lives Matter movement, struggles against settler colonialism in Australia, and advocacy for refugees and asylum seekers' rights. The present global context also includes devastating wildfires, tornadoes, hurricanes, floods, and other disasters, as well as new and protracted conflicts and wars. These global patterns – the climate emergency, the pandemic, and protests against systemic and structural injustices – are deeply interconnected. This context has influenced the shape of this book and makes its contribution to development thinking all the more salient, and urgent.

This introduction outlines the approach we take in the book: our understanding of development and the lens we use to interrogate development discourse and practices. Crucially, development does not exist as a thing or an endpoint. Rather, it is a series of relations between places, social groups, cultures, humans and non-humans, and spheres of production and consumption. Escobar (1995: 87) explains that these relations 'established between institutions, socio-economic processes, forms of knowledge, technological factors and so on – define the conditions under which objects, concepts, theories and strategies can be incorporated into the [development] discourse'. Consequently, Development Studies attempts to understand how these relations are produced, the forms they take, and their effects, and to examine the policies and interventions devised to address the inequalities caused by these relations.

This book adopts a critical approach that challenges the dominant, modernist, and ahistorical narratives often rehearsed in development discourse, policies, and practices. It foregrounds the concealed, critical discourses that are largely written out of conventional development histories or that have been marginalised in the mainstream accounts that influence contemporary understandings. Our global, historical critique of ideas and practices of development is grounded in critical interpretations advanced by, for example, postcolonial, decolonial, and feminist perspectives and analyses.

Meanings of development

While the term *development* is ubiquitous, it is also conceptually and geographically fluid, dynamic, and contested, spurring endless debates about what exactly 'development' means. In *Power of Development*, Jonathan Crush (1995: 6) explains why defining development can be so complicated:

> the [development] machine is global in its reach, encompassing departments and bureaucracies in colonial and post-colonial states throughout the world, Western aid agencies, multilateral organisations, the sprawling global network of NGOs (non-governmental organisations), experts and private consultants, private sector organisations such as banks and companies that marshal the rhetoric of development, and the plethora of Development Studies programs in institutes of learning worldwide.

His words attest to the complexity, diversity, and scope of development. Additionally, Crush illustrates the challenges of locating the complex (at times conflictual) spatial, temporal, and agential boundaries of development. The diverse range of actors and agents involved in development ideas and action often promote contradictory priorities, policies, and practices. Defining development is further complicated since concepts, ideas, and approaches are continuously evolving and shifting.

One fundamental problem in defining development is the confusion 'between the idea of development as purposeful intervention and development as outcome' (Lewis 2019: 1957). David Lewis discusses the varied and changing meanings of development, arguing that 'confusion arises because the word "development" is sometimes used to refer to change and its consequences, while other times it refers to the intentions of institutional actors to bring about change' (2019: 1957). Michael Cowen and Robert W. Shenton (1996) and Gillian Hart (2001) have offered conceptual interventions to address this discrepancy. Cowen and Shenton call for historical enquiry into 'the invention of development' as both an idea and a practice. To address the ambiguities surrounding development as unfolding societal change and development 'as a goal of action', they propose a distinction between development as an 'immanent process' and 'intentional practice' (1996: 3).

Hart offers a similar distinction between 'little d' and 'big D' development. 'Big D' Development describes the Western intervention and modernisation projects in the 'Third World' that emerged during the post-World War II period and the Cold War in newly independent countries. On the other hand, 'little d' development is understood as the 'development of capitalism … a geographically uneven, profoundly contradictory set of historical processes' (Hart 2001: 650). 'Little d' development produces inequalities and struggles for power and resources, while Development denotes development agencies' conscious efforts to intervene and promote positive change within these wider societal shifts. The 'D/d' concept informs debates about theory and practice in development, and challenges managerial and technical approaches that pay insufficient attention to politics, context, and history (Lewis 2019). Hart's distinction allows for a more historicised analysis of contemporary neoliberal capitalism and global power, and potentially helps us challenge dominant discourses and construct alternative development paths (see also Hart 2010).

However, as Lewis (2019: 5) laments, the term 'development' is often not conceptually unpacked *à la* Cowen and Shenton and Hart. Rather, it refers to a variety of economic and social transformations, and the ideas of 'progress' they contain. It can also describe the policies, interventions, and activities of aid agencies, NGOs, and development practitioners. This conflation obscures the multiple and varied meanings of development. However, in practice, it is often difficult to distinguish between development as intentional modernisation interventions from the mid-20th century onwards and development as wider processes of socio-economic change.

As Mawdsley and Taggart (2022) convincingly argue, the relationship between d and D development is increasingly hybridised: 'under conditions of deepening and evolving state capitalism, little "d" development is no longer merely contained by Development. Rather, the actors, goals and logics that constitute "development" now also inhabit the Development sector, including its governance, institutions, narratives, personnel and agendas' (2022: 20). Moreover, modernisation and development interventions have always incorporated individuals and communities into unfolding capitalist relations to reproduce and embed systems of power. While development is a politically powerful discourse, it is also relentlessly material, catalysing substantial social transformations. The discussions throughout this book are underpinned by concerns about how such power, knowledge, and control manifest and are exercised between individuals, collectives, and nations. We adopt a critical, historical approach, explained in more detail below, to reveal global inequalities, examine the reproduction of global spatial and temporal divisions, and identify emerging spaces for more progressive ways forward.

Our approach: centring critical perspectives

In this book, we embrace an unashamedly critical approach to development. We see this as essential for exposing the limits and effects of development, as construed, and finding lacunae from which progressive possibilities for change can emerge. As Silvey and Rankin (2011: 1) write, 'the strength of recent critical development studies lies in its capacity to connect analysis of the violence and exclusion characteristic of both old and new imperialist geographies with practical and normative commitments to the creation and sustenance of spaces of political possibility'. Such critiques of orthodox theories and practices have, until relatively recently, been largely excluded from mainstream development discourse. While there have undoubtedly been significant and profound intellectual shifts in the global development landscape, critical reflections continue to be salient. Importantly, we are wary of the assumption that development is fundamentally, in all places and at all times, founded upon humanitarian principles. Instead, as other critical scholars have shown, development is often a site of ongoing contestation and oppression (see Ferguson 1990; Mignolo 2011; Mosse 2005; Quijano 2000).

We further explore how development discourses and practices are being reshaped and how dominant Western framings of development are beginning to fade. Since the early 2000s, an increasingly multipolar development landscape has emerged, brought about by growing involvement of the so-called rising powers. These countries, collectively known as the BRICS (Brazil, Russia, India, China, South Africa), have gained global economic and political power and now challenge Eurocentric development norms, values, and approaches. Some scholars argue that this 'southernisation of development' has led to new spatialities of development and ruptured the 'formerly dominant North–South axis of power and knowledge' (Mawdsley 2018: 172).

The expansion of South–South cooperation, the transmission of knowledge, resources, and technology between developing countries, is often 'set within claims to shared colonial and post-colonial experiences and anchored within a wider framework of promoting the collective strength of the "South"' (Mawdsley 2020: 227). This cooperation was initially characterised by technical assistance, humanitarian aid, and social programs. However, many Southern partners, particularly China, now place greater emphasis on economic growth as the main driver of development. This takes varied forms, such as investments in physical infrastructure, information and communications technologies, and energy production and manufacturing. China's 'South–South' internationalisation 'is most visible in the Belt and Road Initiative (BRI), which was initiated in 2013 and has subsequently morphed into a multi-stranded geopolitical and geo-economic project' (Mohan 2021: 54).

While significant shifts in the spatialities of the development landscape are now widely acknowledged, the involvement and contribution of the rising powers continues to be hotly debated in Development Studies (see Jepson 2020; Li et al. 2021). The focus of much of this discussion has been the extent to which the move towards more diffuse, complex, and connected global relations has diminished the dominance of Western development. Mignolo suggests that, although it is becoming increasingly difficult for the West to impose its will over 'the rest', conflicts arise 'between dewesternization and the response to it being mounted by the West: namely, rewesternization, the effort to not lose the privileges acquired over the past five hundred years' (2018: xiii). Mohan (2021: 71) also contends that this increasingly multipolar world continues to promote the development of 'racialized, power-laden capitalism'.

Mignolo distinguishes between multipolarity and pluriversity to understand these complexities and conflicts and to illustrate the form and extent of the tenacity of the North–South axis. While state-led de-Westernisation forges a multipolar world order, only decoloniality can open the horizon for a pluriversal world (Mignolo 2018: xii):

> I would like to use pluriversity in the sphere of the decolonial projects emerging out of the global political society (deracializing and depatriarchizing projects, food sovereignty, reciprocal economic organization and the definancialization of money, decolonization of knowledge and of being, decolonization of religion as a way to liberate spirituality, decolonization of aesthetics as a way to liberate esthesis, etc.) and multipolarity in the sphere of politico-economic dewesternization, led by state projects.

This understanding of the pluriverse, a concept we return to later, highlights important challenges to Eurocentric framings of development and the historical assumptions underpinning them. It also acknowledges the growing recognition and inclusion of Indigenous voices and perspectives. Indigenous and non-Western scholars' perspectives, which have long been marginalised in academia, encourage a rethinking of the world from multiple perspectives and produce epistemic and ontological diversity. As such, critical approaches (like the one adopted in this book) demand serious and thorough engagement with Indigenous knowledges and non-Western ontologies. Such knowledges offer crucial insight into the processes that create and reproduce poverty and inequality, unequal power relations, domination and exploitation, and environmental degradation. They also foster possibilities to move beyond dominant Eurocentric constructions and practices of development through alternative, sustainable, and relevant versions and visions of change. This rethinking must begin with historical analysis. Without an understanding of past injustices, the present will remain incomprehensible, and our ability to challenge present-day inequalities will be forever constrained.

Historical perspective: colonial legacies and decoloniality

Our critical, historical approach responds to recent calls to decolonise knowledge, research, and the academy – including Development Studies. This effort requires situating present-day development within its historical and, specifically, colonial legacy. The evolution of development ideologies and narratives over time is well charted (Jolly and Santos 2016; Ziai 2017); however, this history of development is often rehearsed as a unilinear, singular trajectory. With a few notable exceptions, the history of development tends towards compartmentalisation whereby clearly bounded, successive periods characterised by specific theoretical hegemonies create a singular, linear trajectory. Typically, the story begins with economic growth and modernisation theories before discussing theories of 'underdevelopment' and culminating in the Washington Consensus and neoliberalism (see Hettne 1995; Preston 1996). This periodisation is then mapped onto particular events and processes. For example, 1945 is often reified as the year development was invented, due to the founding of the World Bank, United Nations (UN), and other Bretton Woods institutions. We must challenge these conventional genealogies that obscure the colonial legacies of development, and alternative attempts of worldmaking, such as those that constitute the New Economic International Order (Getachew 2019), and that limit attempts at decoloniality embedded in more radical aspects of the origins of development.

This book contributes to the important work already underway to decolonise Development Studies and explore how the field can move beyond its complicity with the imperial project. We argue that tracing development's multiple and extended histories and exploring the potential of decolonial scholarship are necessary starting points for the decolonisation of development and Development Studies. We hope this book makes a valuable contribution towards decolonising knowledge and stimulating new thinking about development.

Spatial and temporal demarcations

This book also challenges the crude spatial distinctions that demarcate where development should take place. Such imaginaries ascribe particular characteristics to different societies to legitimise certain people intervening in the lives of others. The (earlier) reductive geographies of development are now being reconfigured, including foundational spatial binaries, such as 'developed' and 'underdeveloped' regions, 'first' and 'third' worlds, and donors and beneficiaries. There is a growing recognition that development is a global issue, not only a problem for 'certain parts' of the world. For instance, poverty, inequality, and environmental change cannot be addressed by a single country or region. Additionally, large-scale transnational movements, detention, and resettlement of people fleeing violence and persecution are global issues demanding a global humanity, solidarity, responsibility, and response. These insights are replete with progressive potential and have led some scholars to suggest a shift away from *International* and toward *Global* Development (see Horner and Hulme 2019; Horner 2020; Hope et al. 2021). However, we must remain mindful that, even as the processes of global development connect us all, the impacts of global economic, political, and social forces, historically and geographically defined and reproduced in the present day, result in very different outcomes for different people and places (Global Development Studies 2018).

Besides identifying and challenging these spatial distinctions and borders, this book examines how different conceptualisations, imaginings, and uses of time and temporality shape global inequalities. To date, little work has considered how Western discourses of time, and temporal distinctions between the past, present, and future, are used to characterise contemporary societies, distinguish between people and places, and produce a spatial mapping of different temporalities. Such conceptual divisions are perhaps most noticeable in the future-oriented international aid industry, where notions of modernity articulate a singular, universal trajectory of progress that identifies certain people and places as pre-modern or 'left behind'. Temporalities of 'past', 'present', and 'future' are not only associated with historical moments, but also with particular people and places. This constructs spatio-temporal distance between the 'here and now' of the West and the 'there and then' of the so-called Third World, which is framed as less modern, underdeveloped, and existing in the 'past'. Unsettling these problematic uses of temporality creates a space for alternative understandings of time to emerge.

Studying development

The study of development is inseparable from development discourse, practice, and interventions and from wider processes of 'imminent' change. Bruce Currie-Alder (2016: 7) suggests that, 'at its core, Development Studies combines both concern over the existence of poverty within society (the have-nots) [with] the quest to understand and shape how society changes over time'.

Development Studies is interdisciplinary; it draws on anthropology, economics, sociology, politics, political economy, political ecology, psychology, history, geography, and other disciplines beyond the social sciences. It also embraces ontological diversity beyond academic 'disciplines', including Indigenous knowledges and research from various development agencies. Ultimately, it combines a variety of theoretical, methodological, and analytical approaches to understand cultural, political, economic, environmental, and social change. Therefore, Development Studies aims to explain complex processes of societal transformations occurring within and across multiple scales (i.e. from local to global) from historical and contemporary perspectives. While Development Studies historically only centred the 'problems' of poorer, developing nations in Africa, Asia, and Latin America, its mandate has since expanded. The field now investigates development issues wherever they arise.

Development Studies offers a space for normative, moral, and value-based concerns, and an opportunity for critical self-reflection on ethical issues and the politics of representation. Researchers and students in Development Studies are often motivated by concerns for social justice, solidarity, and mutual respect between diverse peoples and cultures, and a desire to reflect these concerns in academic debates (Global Development Studies 2018). Additionally, feminist, decolonial, and postcolonial analyses have forged a space for alternative narratives and voices of the (previously) marginalised. However, inequalities in academia persist and, as Wilson (2001: 214) reminds us, we must pursue a 'more critical understanding of the underlying assumptions, motivations and values that inform research practices'.

Scope, structure, and organisation of the book

This book does not follow a conventional chronological structure of development that maps Global North-centric events one after the other. Instead, each chapter begins by reviewing orthodox understandings and histories of the selected theme before deliberating on how critical thinking can contribute new insights to current debates and offer progressive ways forward.

The next chapter discusses the emergence and progression of development discourses, theories, and practices. It challenges singular, unilinear, and chronological versions by detailing the co-existence of different ideas that complicate what development means and how it is practised. The chapter also summarises economic growth and social development approaches. These have long been central tenets of development and continue to demarcate how development is defined, measured, and practised. Chapter 3 further develops this critique by analysing how people and places are classified. It examines the spatial, temporal, and disciplinary boundaries that demarcate and delimit development research, policy, and interventions. It identifies the 'where' (spatial bordering) and the 'who' of development (i.e. different actors and agents involved in the development industry). We then discuss how problematic representations of places and people in the Global South impact development practice. While Chapters 2 and 3 critique mainstream development history, theories, and representations, Chapter 4 offers critical ideas and approaches that can advance new, more radical directions for development. Specifically, this chapter focuses on postcolonial, feminist, and post-development contributions, including the significance of Indigenous ontologies and decoloniality in development thinking.

While Chapters 2, 3, and 4 examine how key areas of development interventions are theorised, planned, and practised in the context of contemporary global change, Chapter 5 moves on to consider the three central pillars or promises of development – employment, health, and education. It examines the institutions that promote these development priorities, particularly how such promises are approached and the persistent challenges of achieving them. Chapter 6 discusses the relationship between migration, (im)mobility, and development. It conceptualises migrants and migration before introducing the migration–development nexus. The chapter then examines how recent interventions in critical migration and mobility studies, as well as decoloniality, can revise our understandings of migration in the context of development. Chapter 7 explores the pressing global challenge of climate change and environmental sustainability. It interrogates the problematic relationship between degradation and development and reviews critical approaches that can more effectively address issues of environmental sustainability. The book concludes in Chapter 8 by suggesting ways forward for a decolonial development, including discussions of revised notions of solidarity and considerations of the pluriverse.

Given the multiplicity of (often interchangeable) terms used in development discourse, it is important to provide a note on terminology before proceeding. As Solarz (2017: 1793) writes:

> it was from the 1940s onwards that all the spatial terms used today to describe the world in terms of diversity of development were coined. Without them, any attempt to characterise the contemporary international community is impossible. And with them, given their history, associations and content, this task is beset with problems of misconception and miscommunication.

The terms 'Global North' and 'Global South' are currently in vogue. They represent an attempt to move away from the hierarchical, patronising, and divisive perceptions invoked by 'First World' and 'Third World'. Yet, these terms also depict imprecise distinctions between people and places and assume depoliticised geographical descriptors that conceal global inequalities founded upon dispossession, colonialism, and alterity (see Müller 2020; Reuveny and Thompson 2007). Furthermore, there are many populations in the Global North who can relate to Global South experiences (e.g. migrants and diasporas, Indigenous populations under settler colonial regimes). While acknowledging that all terminology fixes and divides, we follow Müller (2020: 735) in purposely deploying 'Global South' terminology to signify an epistemological approach that is 'part and parcel of the postcolonial project of making the subaltern speak'.

Development is a vast, complex, and diverse area of study and practice. It is impossible to cover its many complexities, subfields, and histories in a short book such as this. Instead, the text offers some ways to guide and direct forms of change without reproducing colonial forms of representation, power, and control. We aim to move beyond simply critiquing colonialism; we also challenge the claims of universality evident in much critical scholarship. In so doing, we respond to Escobar (2018), Mignolo (2011), and others who call for an embrace of a pluriverse of non-Western values, perspectives, and societies. This effort requires fundamentally rethinking the relationships between knowledge and power. In this context, we suggest that development, and the achievement of global social justice, require a more affective endeavour that forges practices of care and justice. Development discourse and practice must remain cognisant of how historically unequal relations continue to be reproduced today. We hope that this book helps enable not-fully-mobilised critiques, and illuminates still-obscured histories and ways of knowing.

2 Mainstream development histories and ideas

This chapter reviews the emergence of global development and the interdisciplinary field of Development Studies, which frames, shapes, and transgresses understandings of development. We critique the partial, mainstream versions of the history of development and explore how previous theoretical traditions continue to influence present-day development ideas and practices. In so doing, this chapter draws attention to the extensive relationship between colonialism and the post-independence development industry. We review how the dominant theories underpinning development continue to demarcate how development is defined, measured, and practised.

Until the early 2000s, with few notable exceptions (Crush 1995; Escobar 1995; Grillo and Stirrat 1997), the history of development in research and teaching was often rehearsed through successive, compartmentalised, and clearly bounded periods characterised by specific theories. This singular and linear account typically begins with economic growth and modernisation theories, then discusses theories of underdevelopment, followed by neoliberalism and the Washington Consensus (see Hettne 1995; Preston 1996), and culminating with inclusive development and the UN Development Goals. This periodisation is mapped onto particular events and processes and often reifies 'the beginning of development' with the establishment of the World Bank and other Bretton Woods institutions in 1945. An alternative, political economy version traces the history of development by decade: the golden years of the 1950s, import substitution industrialisation in the 1960s, the debt crisis of the 1970s, structural adjustment programmes (SAPs) in the 1980s, alternative development and the Millennium Development Goals in the 1990s, and the Sustainable Development Goals from the mid-2010s. Since the 1990s, critical development perspectives have challenged these orthodox chronologies (Kothari and Minogue 2001; Marchand and Parpart 1995; Rist

1997); however, even alternative versions sometimes conform to similar periodisations (Munck and O'Hearn 1999; Rahnema and Bawtree 1997).

One reason for these rather abbreviated versions of the emergence of development, and its explicitly post-war start date, is the perceived need to distance development thought and practice from Western imperial history. Concealing the colonial past and installing a temporal boundary forge, perhaps unwittingly, a distinction between 'bad' colonialism of the past (exploitative, extractive, and oppressive) and present-day 'good' development (moralistic, philanthropic, and humanitarian). This distancing from colonialism effectively absolves those working in and on development from addressing how their ideas and practices are associated with various forms of colonial rule, authority, and inequality. Bounded classifications and epochal historicisations undermine attempts to illustrate historical continuities, acknowledge ongoing critiques, and identify divergences in development theory and practice. The limited historical analysis is exacerbated by the largely unreflexive, future-oriented nature of the field, as exemplified by the international development industry's imperative to achieve UN Development Goal targets. Such universal goals and targets not only ignore the historical relationship between colonialism and development but also prescribe a predetermined future. Countering these trends requires developing longer historical perspectives and alternative readings of the origins and evolution of development.

This chapter reviews the emergence and growth of Development Studies while exploring how mainstream disciplinary histories can be subverted beyond the simple periodisation of theoretical positions. In departing from conventional histories, we avoid a unilinear, chronological evolution. Rather, we emphasise the co-existence of different ideas to blur and complicate meanings and practices of development. We review the origins of the field of Development Studies and identify how imperialism, empire, and settler colonialism have influenced contemporary development. Many scholars now acknowledge that Development Studies (and other social sciences and humanities disciplines) is founded on Eurocentric understandings of the world and has long neglected non-Western insights and contributions. There is also a growing recognition that Western forms of knowledge seeking to know, explain, and model the world (e.g. about the economy, democracy, development, education, culture, and racial difference) are neither objective nor universal, despite being promoted as such. Instead, they effectively silence other critically important knowledge and practices.

Colonial genealogies of development: imperialism, empire, and settler colonialism

The origins of contemporary development are situated in colonialism. More profoundly, colonial rule, oppression, and destabilisation hindered the development of colonised people and places, sometimes for centuries. In the ground-breaking text *How Europe Underdeveloped Africa*, Walter Rodney (1972) argued that exploitation by European imperialists directly led to the contemporary underdevelopment of most African nations. Additionally, the transatlantic slave trade, plantation slavery, and colonisation were integral to Europe's industrial revolution (Williams 1944; Robinson 2000; Wilson 2012).

This process of underdevelopment is evidenced, for example, by British imperialism in India. In 1810, India exported more textiles to England than it imported; however, by 1830, this flow of trade had reversed. The British erected prohibitive tariff barriers that effectively shut out manufactured goods from India. Meanwhile, commodities from Britain were still sent to India, a practice backed by British military force. Additionally, imperial ideology was intricately tied to notions of a colonial 'humanity' that sought to draw people subjected to colonial rule out of their 'Asiatic darkness' and bring about Western Enlightenment. Britain 'provided' India with political institutions and citizens based on the British model. Imperialists claimed that they were expanding civilisation to underdeveloped countries and justified their military and technological strength with beliefs in their racial and cultural superiority.

European colonisation was founded on the dispossession and expropriation of land, resources, and labour. Since these processes were spatially and temporally varied, colonised people experienced colonialism in diverse and multiple ways. For example, Europeans proletarianised some Indigenous populations to exploit their labour to fund the empire; however, when colonisers only wanted access to land, not labour, Indigenous people were systematically decimated. Such extermination and elimination were most evident in settler colonies, where colonial power was primarily directed towards removing First Nations people from their land (Coulthard 2014). Since first contact, European settlers have engaged in an ongoing dual process of dissolving Indigenous societies through murder, genocide, or assimilation and by establishing new settler societies on expropriated land (Wolfe 2006).

Historically, Indigenous people were violently eliminated through massacres, forced starvation, poisoning, rape, disease, and incarceration (Reynolds 1996). Attempts to change subjectivities, behaviours, beliefs, and values through assimilation also played a role in the acquisition of land. First Nations people have what Kānaka Maoli scholar Noelani Goodyear-Ka'ōpua terms, 'land-centered literacies' 'based on an intimate connection with and knowledge of the land' (Goodyear-Ka'ōpua 2013: 30). Therefore, assimilation was a long-term strategy aimed at reducing resistance to ongoing settler expansion by changing Indigenous norms into more amenable settler ways of thinking.

The age of formal European empires crumbled in three main phases. First, most Latin American countries gained independence from Spain and Portugal between 1808 and 1826. Second, the settler colonies of Canada (1867), Australia (1900), and South Africa (1910) were granted dominion status. Third, nationalist and independence movements, coupled with the economic and political consequences of World War II, led to the large-scale dismantling of Western European empires from the late 1940s. However, political sovereignty and national independence did not end all forms of colonialism. Neo-colonialism, coloniality, and processes of re-colonisation continue to sustain present-day global economic, political, and social interests. Therefore, while formal independence marked a crucial point in the transition away from direct colonial rule, indirect imperial control persists. Edward Said (1989) aptly summarises the ongoing legacies of colonial technologies and forms of knowledge:

> To have been colonised was a fate with lasting, indeed grotesquely unfair results, especially after national independence had been achieved. Poverty, dependency, underdevelopment, various pathologies of power and corruption, plus of course notable achievements in war, literacy, economic development: this mix of characteristics designated the colonised people who had freed themselves on one level but who had remained victims of their past on another. (207)

Moreover, Godlewska and Smith (1994: 268) warn that, 'it would be a mistake to conclude that … de-colonisation marked the end of empire. It did effectively signal an end to colonialism as a specific form of empire, but imperial interest and global reach continue to the present'.

The legacy of colonialist thinking remains embedded in development ideas (Miege 1980). Goldsmith (1997) argues that development reproduces a form of unequal trade reminiscent of colonial economic control and exploitation. Similarly, Mamdani (1996, 2020) located continuities (and some divergences) in colonial and present-day institutional, governance, and administrative systems, while Cooke (2003) links continuities between contemporary development management and colonial administration. Colonial legacies also exist in other areas of contemporary development such as participatory approaches (Cooke and Kothari 2001), gender and development (McEwan 2001; Mohanty 2003; Parpart 1995; Radcliffe 1994), community development, and conservation development (Adams and Mulligan 2002).

This historical continuum, from colonialism to development, can also be seen in various articulations of modernity and progress. Colonialism was not simply an economic project; it culturally created and maintained classifications and hierarchies between groups of people (Dirks 1992). Dichotomies of, for example, 'modern' and 'traditional' or the 'West' and the 'rest' (Hall and Gieben 1992) remain embedded within development discourses and colonial classifications of difference are often invoked to justify development interventions. This representation, that peoples in and of the 'Third World' need to be developed, reflects global distinctions established during the colonial period when colonised people were envisaged as 'backwards', 'traditional', and incapable of self-government.

The decline of European empires meant that by 1980, 100 newly independent nations had been inducted into the UN. The decline in European empires also heralded the ascension of the US to a position of world hegemony – a change only contested by the Soviet Union at the time. We now turn to this post-WWII period.

Modernisation, coloniality, and the emergence of post-war development

Though many countries have gained independence and the period of direct colonial rule has all but ceased, patterns of dispossession and structures of inequality established during the colonial period continue to define the post-independence and post-war development era (Mignolo 2021; Quijano 2000; Walsh 2020). This process of coloniality orders relations based on perceived differences and hierarchies and structures and controls labour, resources, and modes of production (Quijano 2000) that do not subscribe to Western norms (Maldonado-Torres 2007). Global processes of development perpetuate these relations by identifying and intervening in the lives of those perceived to need improvement. In this way, colonial relations have shifted from direct oppression and exploitation to promoting and exporting Western ideals of modern-isation and progress; therefore, these altered and amended practices cannot be seamlessly mapped onto development ideals. Anticolonial activist and first President of Ghana, Kwame Nkrumah, warned in his text *Neo-Colonialism, the Last Stage of Imperialism* (1965) that:

> Neo-colonialism is also the worst form of imperialism. For those who practise it, it means power without responsibility, and for those who suffer from it, it means exploitation without redress. In the days of old-fashioned colonialism, the imperial power had at least to explain and justify at home the actions it was taking abroad. In the colony those who served the ruling Imperial power could at least look to its protection against any violent move by their opponents. With neo-colonialism neither is the case. (xi)

The starting point of modern-day development is often attributed to US President Truman's 1949 inauguration speech. In his speech, Truman articulated a blueprint for the West's modernising mission in the Global South:

> we must embark on a bold new program for making the benefits of our sci-entific advances and industrial progress available for the improvement and growth of underdeveloped areas ... More than half the people of the world are living in conditions approaching misery. Their food is inadequate. They are victims of disease. Their economic life is primitive and stagnant. Their poverty is a handicap and a threat both to them and to more prosperous areas. For the first time in history, humanity possesses the knowledge and the skill to relieve the suffering of these people ... The United States is pre-eminent among nations in the development of industrial and scientific techniques. The mate-

rial resources which we can afford to use for the assistance of other peoples are limited. But our imponderable resources in technical knowledge are constantly growing and are inexhaustible. (President Truman, 20 January 1949)

Truman depicted the Global South as 'underdeveloped' and appealed for whole societies to be saved by Western, and specifically US, technology, infrastructure, worldviews, and ideology. For Truman, the level of technological innovation in the US and other Western countries indicated civility and progressiveness. Such innovation and infrastructure could, therefore, be exported to Global South countries to help them 'catch up' and modernise (Sachs 2006).

After the devastating wars of the first half of the 20th century, development and its interventions were seen as tools to deliver modernisation to the world, in what Tania Li (2007) has termed the 'will to improve'. Initially, interventions focused on infrastructural and technical fixes. However, development also began to undertake social and cultural shifts that shaped the subjectivities, aspirations, and behaviours of those being modernised. The meanings and goals of post-war development were rooted in specific theories and approaches. The following sections examine two specific foundational approaches to development. First, we discuss the long-privileged primary goal of economic growth. We then examine human development approaches that attempted to make the economic more social.

Development as economic growth

The origins of economic development are generally attributed to the work of Adam Smith (1723–90). Modern economic development still relies on his theorisation of the role of the market in economic growth. Smith's (1776) notion of the division of labour argues that productivity will increase if different people concentrate their labour on different components of the production process and, thus, become skilled in these specific aspects of production. Smith's contemporary, Ricardo (1772–1823), added a spatial dimension to this division of labour in his theory of free trade and 'comparative advantage'. Instead of concentrating on divisions between individuals, Ricardo (1912) believed that entire countries should focus on producing goods based on their relative advantages (i.e. specific assets, such as land, mineral resources, labour, and technical and scientific expertise). Countries should not attempt to produce everything and any-thing; rather, they must strategically specialise to make production more efficient within this global division of labour (Ricardo 1912). However, in reality, countries that produced raw materials benefited far less than those manufacturing raw materials into higher-value commodities. This unequal relationship was articulated by the Singer–Prebisch thesis, which suggests that, over the long term, the price of primary commodities, such as coffee beans, coal, and cotton, would decline relative to the price of manufactured goods, such as clothing and cars, and ultimately lead to the deterioration of primary-product-based economies. Therefore, 'compar-ative advantages' effectively benefit the West, while the Global South faces a comparative disadvantage.

Smith and Ricardo believed the market was the most efficient mechanism to maximise resource use and improve human well-being. They assumed that greater economic wealth would lead to benefits such as improved health and education. However, significant economic events, such as the 1929 Wall Street crash and the Great Depression of the 1930s in the United States, led many to question the ability of the free market to achieve broad prosperity, and economists began to develop new, alterna-tive understandings of economic development.

John Maynard Keynes (1883–1946) was a key figure in questioning whether the free market was the most direct path to economic growth. He believed that the key to growth was investment in state infrastructure, which would lead to job creation and wealth generation. For Keynes (1973), the state was central to economic growth and governments should intervene in the market to encourage investment, especially through direct government expenditure. Keynes was a key advisor to the British government during World War II and Keynesianism influenced post-war reconstruction of Europe, informing the economic develop-ment policies of various international organisations in their attempts to rehabilitate, stabilise, and control the global economy. The World Bank, International Monetary Fund (IMF), and International Bank for Reconstruction and Development were formed at the Bretton Woods conferences in 1944–47. These institutions were created to support the rebuilding of post-war economies and foster international economic cooperation among nations. In the words of Keynes (1944), 'it was a shift away from the tacit, convention-based cooperation of central bankers to a sweeping, rule-based multilateral cooperation of states' which sought 'a common measure, a common standard, a common rule applicable to each and not irksome to any'. However, many scholars have since argued that the Bretton Woods institutions are 'protectionist, asymmetrical and impede balanced economic development' in part because their 'governance structure was comprised largely of industrialised countries who often took decisions that benefited themselves to the disadvantage of newly independent nations' (Igwe 2018: 121).

In the post-war period, most multilateral agencies and governments in the Global North believed 'development' could be achieved through variations on the Keynesian approach, including national-level government interventions and foreign aid assistance. For example, the United States' Marshall Plan channelled aid to fund Europe's reconstruction and arguably became the dominant touchstone for development throughout the 1950s and 1960s (Todaro and Smith 2015). Subsequently, development was defined as a series of successive stages of economic growth as articulated in Rostow's *The Stages of Economic Growth: A Non-Communist Manifesto* (1990). Rostow distinguished between 'more developed' and 'less developed' regions using 'stages of economic growth' on the way to the final stage, 'High Mass Consumption'.

In the 1950s, development economics was framed as a way to rescue 'the people of the poor countries from their poverty' (Galbraith 1979, cited in Escobar 1988: 432). However, by the 1960s and 1970s, economic development models were clearly failing to address poverty in the Global South, while aiding growth and accumulation in the Global North. Economic growth did not trickle down and was not sustaining social development as income inequalities between countries continued to widen. A subsequent disillusionment with modernisation fuelled thinking from the Global South, particularly from Latin America (Prebisch 1962).

Dependency theories, or theories of underdevelopment, have long understood underdevelopment as a historical and externally induced phenomenon, not an internal condition of low productivity and poverty (Todaro and Smith 2015). These thinkers argued that development was distorted by relations of dependency (Frank 1966). They saw development as a neo-colonial project of global capitalist expansion that reinforced structures of inequality and reproduced the domination of the South by the

North (see Amin 1976). For example, Julius K. Nyerere (1977), the first President of Tanzania, wrote,

> Equality between nations of the modern world is only a legal equality – it is not an economic reality. Tanzania and America are not equal. A man who needs to sell his labor in order to buy bread and the man who controls both his employment and the price of bread are not equal. Their relationship is one of dependence and dominance. (2)

Underdevelopment was founded on historically unequal trade relations and the international capitalist system. Therefore, development would require a major restructuring of the world capitalist system, not simply internal growth and structural changes (Cohen 1973; Dos Santos 1973). Dependency theorists called attention to international power imbalances and the need for fundamental economic, political, and institutional reforms at domestic and international levels.

Leaders of newly independent states, many of whom played critical roles against former European colonisers, drew on insights from dependency theory to develop 'world making' (Getachew 2019) projects of their own. For example, the New International Economic Order aimed to reorder the global economy towards equity through regulated globalisation with preferential treatment for developing and newly independent states. Getachew (2019: 166) argues that the New International Economic Order aimed for 'a redistribution of rights and obligations in the international order such that the most powerful states shouldered greater burdens for the creation of an egalitarian global economy'.

Despite these challenges and alternatives, the 1980s saw a resurgence of free-market solutions that had been developed from the 1940s onwards (see Hayek 1941; Friedman 1953). This neoliberal ideology redirected development interventions towards market deregulation and individual responsibility (Harvey 2005). Neoliberalism (re-)attributed underdevelopment to inappropriate policies, poor resource allocation, and excessive state intervention (rather than to a structural ordering of global relations to support the development of the Global North). It argued that state intervention in economic activities slows economic growth and invites considerable rent-seeking and corruption (Krueger 1974). Once again, underdevelopment was explained as an internal, domestic problem (Bauer 1984; Lal 1985; Little 1982). The neoliberal 'counter-revolution' challenged the core of Keynesianism, including 'the over-extension of the public sector', 'the over-emphasis of economic policies on investment in physical capital' rather than human capital such as education and health, and 'the widespread use of economic controls, such as tariffs, subsidies, and quotas, which distorted prices' (Toye 1993: 70). It also rejected dependency theories.

Proponents of neoliberalism argue that development should introduce policies to stimulate economic efficiency and economic growth (World Bank 1983). Accordingly, a suite of neoliberal policies, referred to as SAPs, were designed by the World Bank and the IMF in the 1980s and imposed on countries across Africa, South America, and parts of Asia. To receive financial aid to service their debts, Global South governments were compelled to implement these prescribed policies. While the specifics differed between countries, they generally focused on fiscal deficit, monetary policy, privatisation of state assets, and trade liberalisation. However, these policies destabilised many local industries and limited social investment, which deepened economic insecurity and inequality (Herbst 1990; Moseley et al. 2010). Interestingly, structural adjustment ideology also guided economic recovery policies in Italy, Ireland, Spain, Portugal, and Greece during the 2008 Global Financial Crisis (Greer 2014). Yet, even in Europe, the policies resulted in low economic growth, increased unemployment, poverty, and economic inequality (Hermann 2017).

The dominance of the West has debilitated many states and their economies. However, some states have bucked this trend and expanded their economies, namely, China, Brazil, India, Indonesia, South Africa, Nigeria, and Mexico. China's growth, in particular, now rivals that of the US. China now leads various development interventions to promote its global dominance and offer an alternative to Western aid. Unlike Western developmentalism, China funds development projects without interfering in domestic issues. For instance, the Belt and Road Initiative (BRI), launched in 2013 by President Xi Jinping, aims to re-establish the Silk Road, a major pre-colonial trading and maritime route linking Eurasia, Oceania, and Africa. The BRI claims to be an example of 'win–win cooperation' that will deliver development and prosperity to Global South countries.

Funds from a Global South country to underwrite development projects in another Global South country are often labelled South–South cooperation. This South–South cooperation 'refers to the transfer and exchange of resources, technology and knowledge, set within claims to shared colonial and post-colonial experiences and identities, and anchored within a wider framework of promoting the collective strength and development of the Global South' (Mawdsley 2019: 259). While some see South–South cooperation as proof of the West's fading dominance in global economic relations, questions remain as to who really benefits. While economic growth, as measured in Gross Domestic Product (GDP), may increase, there are often mixed distributional outcomes. It is unclear whether this growth will translate into structural and sustainable transformation or simply generate new forms of inequality, insecurity, and dispossession. Western hegemony in global economic relations is now challenged by rival advanced economies; however, the logics of economic development continue to be reproduced within the burgeoning Global South economies. Capitalist processes of dispossession and expropriation – once the domain of the West – are now readily adopted by Global South governments (see our discussion on accumulation by dispossession in Chapter 4).

While economic growth remains a central tenet of development, concepts such as social development, well-being, and human rights have gained prominence in recent decades. Such concepts foreground people-centred development and illuminate the inseparable connections between economic and social spheres. These interventions are reviewed in the following section.

Human development: capabilities and freedoms

Starting in the late 1980s, development policy and practice began adopting human development approaches. This supplemented and challenged the long-standing economic development goals that often had disastrous impacts on the social development of populations around the world (Jolly 1991). Economic development approaches had sustained high rates of economic growth for a minority; in contrast, human development approaches envisaged economic growth only as a means to expand people's capabilities and freedoms and improve well-being. This approach went beyond narrowly defined economic development to address the 'full flourishing of all human choices' (United Nations Development Programme [UNDP] 1990) and enable people to lead long and healthy lives, be knowledgeable, and have access to the resources needed for a decent standard of living.

Human development approaches often centred the notion of human capability. The Capability Approach (CA), driven by Amartya Sen, Martha Nussbaum, and others, proposed that development should be assessed based on people's freedom to achieve the functions they 'value and have reason to value' (Sen 2009: 276). Sen (1999: 297) suggests that economic and social policy should exist as 'a process of expanding the substantive freedoms that people have' – that is, their capabilities. Rather than promoting a specific set of capabilities, Sen argues for process freedoms, such as agency and public deliberation, to assist in identifying lists of capabilities for specific social milieus. Sen's (1988: 18) CA only aims to specify 'a space in which evaluation is to take place, rather than proposing one particular formula for evaluation'.

Nussbaum (2006) takes a different approach to Sen, arguing for a broad list of universal capabilities. She believes establishing such a list is necessary since marginalised voices are often ignored by the wider populous, even in democratic processes. Nussbaum suggests that her list of innate capabilities, including those of life, bodily health, bodily integrity, senses, imagination and thought, emotions, practical reason, affiliation, play, and control over one's environment, is broadly relevant to all societies and cultures. Subsequently, other scholars have argued that human development entails more than achieving capabilities. The process of pursuing them must also be equitable, participatory, productive, and sustainable (Streeten 1999). Human development counters other normative development approaches that see economic growth as an end in itself. Rather, human development holds that economic advancement should only be pursued as a means to human well-being.

Since the 1990s, human development approaches have been widely adopted by multilateral development agencies, particularly the UNDP, which launched the annual Human Development Report in 1990. The report includes the Human Development Index (HDI), which measures all nation states along three key indicators (life expectancy, education, and standard of living). This index made significant contributions to global measures of development, which were previously determined using GDP. The HDI better reflects diverse aspects of development by measuring aggregate income and social indicators within and across countries. By measuring average levels of health, education, and income, the HDI purports to offer a more complete picture of the state of a country's development. The Gini coefficient is also used to measure economic inequality by mapping the income distribution of a country's population (or as a combined coefficient for the world).

Debates and discussions around economic growth and human development continue to inform development policies and measurements. While economic and human development approaches were summarised separately here, they often intersect. Their interconnectedness is most evident when considering issues of inequality, where GDP growth and economic stability are framed as important means to achieve and sustain human well-being. Increasing South–South cooperation and the involvement of new regional actors in development also shift the development landscape and devise new approaches to human and economic development. However, as the subsequent chapters show, coloniality, dispossession, and inequalities still persist today.

3 Borders, boundaries, and classifications

International development is based on the foundational distinction that some people and places are developed, and others are not. Development discourse and practice rely on multiple differences and classifications, be they geographical, spatial, material, cultural, or temporal. An array of technologies, practices, and processes forge distinctions between, for example, socio-spatial, ideological, and political regimes that work to divide, exclude, control, govern, and protect. Such ideas are multi-scalar, operating at individual, national, and global levels. However, they are not static; the creating, marking, transgressing, blurring, and dismantling of classifications and borders is a pervasive and ongoing process.

In this chapter, we explore the boundaries demarcating and delimiting development research, policy, and interventions. Distinctions designating certain areas and peoples *for* development are reified through various forms of measurement and representation. Only by reaffirming difference and distance between people and places – between rich and poor, donors and beneficiaries, West and the rest – can the intervening by some in the lives of others be justified. A critical exploration of these bordering and classifying practices is timely and salient, as they continue to order and categorise identities, people, places, knowledge, and landscapes (but are also subject to challenges). This chapter first traces the histories and processes through which different people and places have been, and continue to be, classified and categorised. It then reflects on recent discussions that disrupt the traditional spatial and ideological boundaries of development to support a radical rethinking of development approaches (see Gillespie 2016; Horner and Hulme 2019).

Bordering the discipline

The interdisciplinary field of Development Studies has its origins in colonialism and the last 500 years of European dispossession (Melber 2019). Particular categorisations and classifications emerged from this historical period, identifying some people and places as modern and civilised and others as backward and traditional. Colonialism created classifications and hierarchies between groups of people (Dirks 1992). These deeply racialised distinctions were subsequently mapped onto those identified as developed and underdeveloped, referred to by W.E.B. Du Bois (1903 [2015]: 11) as the global 'colour line'. This legacy of bordering and demarcating created and maintained asymmetries of power and knowledge that resonate in development today. Even a cursory glance at key Development Studies texts reveals the discipline's relationship with and complicity in reinforcing a bordered world that classifies people and places based on perceived levels of modernity, progress, and socio-economic development. Paradoxically, Development Studies is founded upon the very inequalities that it seeks to overcome, the 'imbalances in access to resources that produce "haves" and "have-nots"' (Standing and Taylor 2016: 169).

To understand how and why certain people and places were categorised as inferior, underdeveloped, and uncivilised (and how such narratives justified Western development interventions), we must investigate a longer historical perspective. Therefore, this section illustrates the importance of historical representations to gain a better understanding of the present and, importantly, acknowledge past injustices before moving towards more just development.

The 15th-century 'age of exploration and discovery', beginning in 1492 when Columbus reached North America and 1497 as Vasco da Gama sailed around the Cape of Good Hope, flooded Europe with accounts of so-called newly 'discovered' lands. This knowledge – about animals, plants, people, particular 'races', and parts of the world – was classified, defined, mapped, and categorised. Classificatory ideas were spread through print and exhibition spaces. For example, in London (the heart of Empire), the British Museum, the Natural History Museum, Regents Park Zoo, Kew Gardens, and the Great Exhibition at Crystal Palace in 1851 displayed and categorised expedition findings. As Said (1979: 166) explained, 'regulatory codes, classifications, specimen cases, periodical reviews, dictionaries, grammars, commentaries, editions, translations, all

... formed a *simulacrum* of the Orient and reproduced it materially in the West'.

Racialised representations of 'other' people became widespread and 'common' knowledge. Such classifications masqueraded as dispassionate scientific knowledge, despite being informed by hierarchical, colonialist assumptions, unmediated by the people being described. This is evident in the writings of Henry Stanley. In an 1871 article for the *New York Tribune*, he described his view of a valley near Lake Tanganyika:

> What a settlement one could have in this valley! Fancy a church spire rising where that tamarind rears its dark crown of foliage and think how well a score of pretty cottages would look instead of those thorn clumps and gum trees! How much better would such a state become this valley, rather than its wild and deserted aspect.

Stanley could only imagine the landscape through a Western lens and called for it to be immediately transformed to better resemble the English countryside. Such narratives also reflected the widespread notion that 'Indigenous peoples were habituated and attuned to a static landscape, while Europeans had a more transformative, improving and perfectible relationship with nature' (Lester 2012: 135). People, not just physical landscapes, were represented and interpreted through a hierarchical, racialised colonial discourse. For instance, in North's book (1883) on the people of Seychelles, written for the Royal Botanic Gardens at Kew, she writes, 'nutmeg, cinnamon and cloves were all growing luxuriously, but the natives were too lazy to pick them [and] though many boats went and came ... they were full of dried fish and natives. Equally unpleasant at close quarters' (x).

The places encountered during colonial explorations were often imagined as empty landscapes needing colonial interventions (Phillips 1996). Africa became constructed as the 'Dark Continent' (Stanley 1889), implying a need to explore, fill up, and make known. It was seen as 'a primeval, bestial, reptilian, or female entity to be tamed, enlightened, guided, opened, and pierced by white European males through Western science, Christianity, civilization, commerce, and colonialism' (Jarosz 1992: 110). Notably, colonial maps marked swathes of the world as *terra nullius* – land deemed unoccupied, uninhabited, and belonging to no one. This is particularly true in settler colonialism. For example, British colonial rule in Australia (and subsequent Australian land laws) was premised on the claim of *terra nullius*. It justified British occupation, without treaty or payment, and effectively denied Indigenous people's prior connection to the land. *Terra nullius* was only legally rejected in Australia in 1992 following the high-profile Mabo court case.

Racist representations were deeply informed by theories of Social Darwinism and its claims of survival of the fittest. This was intensified through the regressive ideology of eugenics, which discouraged procreation between people with so-called 'unwanted human traits' and encouraged the ideal traits of whiteness and behaviours associated with the European elite. Eugenics ideology informed policies, such as the 'White Australian Policy', an immigration policy in the early 1900s that sought to govern a 'breeding pool' of the ideal 'white' worker. The construction of race as a biological trait was mobilised to 'breed out' Indigenous people by assimilating and integrating them into settler societies.

Imperial interventions and expansionist policies were legitimised by representations of people and cultures, so-called empty landscapes, and notions of white superiority. Such interventions were 'justified in defence of humanitarianism' (Lester 2002: 133), a civilising mission, or the 'white man's burden' (Kipling 1899). Of course, conquest and colonisation were never humanistic, but exercises in violence and dispossession. As James Baldwin writes in *No Name in the Street* (2007: 85), 'all of the Western nations have been caught in a lie, the lie of their pretended humanism. This means that their history has no moral justification, and that the West has no moral authority'. Walter Mignolo (2011) suggests that this colonial history is the darker side of Western modernity.

Colonialist policies and views may not seamlessly map onto post-war development discourses. However, historical distinctions, differences, and demarcations (even when changed and adapted) continue to influence contemporary development. For instance, racialised perceptions continue today. Kalpana Wilson (2012) illuminates how white supremacy dehumanises people to uphold structures of power and control over global and local resources and makes mass death and injustice easier to accept. Classifications of people and places permeate knowledge production and continue to shape what we know and how we come to know it. As Cheeseman et al. (2017: 4) remind us, 'differences in research methods and funding between Western and Africanist academia highlight the presence of severe global inequalities in the knowledge economy'. This aspect of neo-colonialism plays out in theory and practice as development workers and academics are, perhaps inadvertently, interpellated by these historical distinctions. Dominant development theories are constructed in the Global North and implemented in the Global South. Western academics and policy makers influence which projects are funded and where aid should be spent or withdrawn. Thus, the power relations between colonisers and those they colonised continue to be reinscribed by contemporary development research and teaching.

Yet, recent endeavours in Development Studies have framed the discipline as flexible, fluid, and contested. Since the 1980s, research and teaching has more readily embraced alternative approaches to development and recognised its problematic genealogy. Some of these critical approaches, explored in more detail in Chapter 4, are introduced below. The next section examines the geographical divisions present in much development discourse, policy, and practice.

The where of development: spatial demarcations

Spatial distinctions in development divide countries into those considered developed and those identified as undeveloped or developing. This distinction has a long and fraught history, most profoundly associated with the partitioning of Africa. At the infamous 1885 Berlin Conference, European leaders carved up Africa for themselves, arbitrarily drawing borders and establishing rules of conquest and trade. They hoped to resolve the growing conflicts over which European powers controlled specific areas, also termed the 'scramble for Africa'. Acemoglu et al. (2001) explain that contemporary African development problems are rooted in the influence and persistence of these colonial divisions, policies, and institutions. As Michalopoulos and Papaioannou (2016: 1804) write, 'the artificial borders fostered ethnic struggles and conflict primarily by splitting groups across the newly minted African states'. Therefore, 'the political geography of colonial Africa had a rationale rooted in colonialism itself but each aspect of it now presents modern Africa with problems' (Griffiths 1986: 204).

More global forms of demarcation are also evident in contemporary spatial framings of development. For instance, countries are often divided based on their levels of economic growth. The World Bank has long used income or Gross National Product (GNP) to classify groups of countries. Some of the earliest categories used to divide nations were 'very poor, poor, middle income and rich' (Reid 1965, quoted in Fantom and Serajuddin 2016: 2). Since 1989, the language has shifted to low-, low-middle-, upper-middle-, and high-income groups. These analytical classifications were primarily used to report levels, trends, and other characteristics of member countries. Importantly, they also divided the world into 'developing' (i.e. low- and low-middle-income) and 'developed' countries (i.e. upper-middle- and high-income). Classifications also determined the form and extent of resource allocation. Significantly, the Organisation for Economic Co-operation and Development's (OECD) Development Assistance Committee (DAC) identifies potential recipients of Official Development Assistance (ODA) based on these distinctions (OECD 2015). However, critics question the rationales of threshold levels for the allocation of resources (Nielsen 2011; Ravallion 2012). An alternative system would link low-income status to a country's internal capacity to eliminate extreme poverty (Ravallion 2009).

Income levels and trends are still used for resource allocation decisions. However, other spatial categories are increasingly used to categorise regions based on their levels of development (Solarz 2017: 1793). While the lexicon may have changed from 'underdeveloped areas' to 'Third World' to 'Global South', 'the spatial reference has remained very consistent' (Horner 2020). Without these distinctions, 'any attempt to characterise the contemporary international community is impossible[, yet] given their history, associations and content, this task is beset with problems of misconception and miscommunication' (Solarz 2017: 1793).

Development discourses and interventions rely on spatial differences (e.g. North/South, First/Third World, industrialised/industrialising, developed/underdeveloped, or rural/urban) to identify where development should occur. These crude distinctions also ascribe particular characteristics to different societies. As such, the 'South', 'developing' or 'Third World' becomes the focus for interventions and the field site for scholarly research; yet, ideology and theory continue to emanate from the North/West. African sites are, at best, considered laboratories or test cases for exploring or verifying the general theories created in the North (Keim 2008). Development generally refers to processes, experiences, and interventions relating to the 'South'. It assumes that the 'South' is an objective reality, defined as the absence of the North. Mawdsley (2017: 108) writes that the '"South" was produced as the disciplinary subject and the "North" as active and benevolent provider of knowledge and material assistance' (see also Kapoor 2008). This reinforces the centrality of Western knowledge, the direction of data, and the sites of knowledge production. Furthermore, the professionalisation of the development industry relies on these boundaries to establish its experts, organisations, and approaches (Kothari 2005).

Challenging spatial borders and new geographies of development

These crude spatial distinctions have proven remarkably durable and persistent, despite challenges from critical scholars (see Kothari 2005; Radcliffe 2005). However, recent reconfigurations of this overarching spatial framework represent significant intellectual shifts in the development landscape. The use of categories to demarcate world regions based on their levels of development is increasingly being disputed (Sidaway 2012). There is growing recognition that poverty, inequality, and development are global phenomena that do not only affect certain parts of the world. Notably, inequalities within countries are increasing (Milanovic 2016) in both the Global North and Global South (International Social Science Council 2016; Ravallion 2014). New geographies of poverty are also being shaped by an increase in the proportion of extreme poverty in middle-income countries (Kanbur and Sumner 2012). Accordingly, some nongovernmental organisations (NGOs) have shifted their work to address inequalities within the Global North.

Moreover, climate and environmental change are clearly global concerns that cannot be solved by a single country or region. The (im)mobility of migrants and refugees and the large-scale transnational movement, detention, and resettlement of people fleeing violence and persecution are also not geographically contained. Additionally, increasing divergences within the Global South and growing South–South cooperation represents 'a paradigmatic shift that both upsets and transcends the old hierarchies of "North" and "South"' (Mawdsley 2017: 112). Mawdsley (2017: 108) considers this to be an 'unprecedented rupture in the North–South axis that has dominated post-1945 international development norms and structures'. Most recently, the global impact of the COVID-19 pandemic confounded spatial boundaries. Some scholars refer to these shifts as a 'great convergence' (Baldwin 2016) that necessitates moving away from the discourse of international development and towards global challenges (Horner and Hulme 2019). As Horner and Hulme (2019: 348–9) write,

> various new geographies of development have been identified since the turn of the millennium, across several spheres such as wealth, middle classes, poverty, health, environment and others … We suggest that, more than at any time over the last century, the contemporary global map of development appears increasingly at odds with any idealized binary notion of a clear spatial demarcation between First and Third Worlds, 'developed' and 'developing', or rich and poor, countries.

Indeed, Horner (2020: 415) suggests that the term 'international development' appears 'increasingly inappropriate for encompassing the various actors, processes, and major challenges with which our world engages in the early 21st Century'. Foundational and longstanding distinctions are becoming blurred. We are entering 'a period of "converging divergence" [with] some narrowing of gaps across countries (from a position of significant departure), and relatively growing significance of greater difference within countries' (Horner and Hulme 2019: 367).

Contemporary times are increasingly referred to as a new global development era. This is most prominently reflected in the United Nations' (UN's) 2015 Sustainable Development Goals (SDGs). In a clear departure from the Millennium Development Goals (MDGs), which focused almost exclusively on targets for developing countries, the SDGs take a global focus to represent the universalisation of development challenges. Additionally, in 2016, the World Bank stated that it would no longer distinguish between developed and developing countries in its annual World Development Indicators (Horner 2020: 416). This decision considered what Horner and Hulme (2019) refer to as the 'converging divergence' between nations, growing concerns around sustainability, and the increasing recognition of global interconnectedness.

We must consider what has actually changed in this new global landscape and the implications for development policy, practice, and discourse. Indeed, Horner (2022) cautions that such shifts may simply involve rebranding, not fundamental changes. Moreover, this framing could downplay historical and contemporary inequalities in the global economic system and conceal racialised and gendered power relations established during colonisation and sustained through ongoing coloniality. However, others welcome the new universal framing of development that removes North–South distinctions. Proponents argue that it focuses on reducing inequalities and building more sustainable, inclusive, and secure futures for all people and societies (Aghajanian and Allouche 2016).

Postcolonial scholarship has long challenged North–South binaries (Radcliffe 2005; Kothari 2007) but on very different historical and political grounds. These scholars highlight 'the contingency of North–South relations; the shifting contexts and contents of Northern views; the varied sites and agents of knowledge; and the complex utility of development to both North and South' (Radcliffe 2005: 293). Furthermore, while the apparent shift from international to global development may be replete with potential, development continues to uphold gendered and racialised divides. There is thus limited convergence of inequality profiles (Milanovic 2016). While the richest countries at the time of the industrial revolution were only three times richer than India and China, the richest countries today are almost 100 times wealthier than the poorest.

Other critics of 'global' development argue from a political economy perspective. For instance, Bram Büscher (2019: 485) contends that Horner and Hulme (2019) do not offer a realistic response to 21st-century development challenges. For Büscher, they do not provide any 'theorisation of what causes these trends, where they come from and what they mean', particularly when it comes to the role of capitalism. From this perspective, capitalist accumulation is the fundamental cause of 21st-century development challenges, so 'we should be working towards "revolutionary development" instead of embracing global development. This involves taking power and politics seriously to (re)imagine radically different development models that allow for structural and systemic change' (Büscher 2019: 492). Such changes must revise 'little d' development (immanent processes of social and economic transformation) and 'big D' development (active intervention; Cowen and Shenton 1996; Hart 2001).

Classifying and categorising the development industry: actors and agents

While spatial demarcations identify the *where* of development, other classifications distinguish between actors and agents (i.e. the form and extent of one's engagement with development). The 'development industry', a phrase coined by Crush (1995), includes a network of multilateral and bilateral institutions, NGOs, and governments, each promoting particular ideologies, regulations, and processes that have, over time, become 'norms' of development. For example, Bretton Woods institutions, such as the World Bank and the International Monetary Fund have long promoted specific types of policies and programs largely linked to economic growth. These priorities are communicated through publications such as the annual World Development Report. UN agencies (e.g. UN Development Program [UNDP], UN Women, UN International Children's Emergency Fund [UNICEF], and UN Environment Programme) also publish reports that focus on their priorities. Notably, the UNDP publishes the Human Development Report, which includes the Human Development Index. Since 1990, this index has challenged development measurements that focus only on economic development; instead, it measures progress using the combined indicators of education, health, and economic growth.

National governments and their aid agencies are also important actors. Development assistance (aid) is regularly tied to specific conditions. These may include employing donor country businesses and technical assistance, advancing the donor country's economic and/or military interests. Even when aid and development assistance are concerned with human well-being, the donor country's interests often inform who is given aid and what it can be used for. This unequal relationship between donor and recipient countries is an enduring feature of the ongoing coloniality of development. However, given the recent decline in aid to low- and middle-income countries, non-aid economic activities such as remittances, foreign direct investment, and trade may ultimately be more influential for most countries.

The development industry also includes philanthropists and corporations seeking to 'give back' through charity and corporate social responsibility. Their entry into development work has been met with both gratitude and scepticism. Some worry that charitable giving simply sidesteps the unequal structures that create wealth accumulation. Even the wealthy sometimes recognise these issues. In a 2013 opinion piece for the *New York Times* titled *The Charitable-Industrial Complex*, Peter Buffett, son and heir to billionaire Warren Buffett, reflected on the inadequacy of charitable giving:

> As more lives and communities are destroyed by the system that creates vast amounts of wealth for the few, the more heroic it sounds to 'give back'. It's what I would call 'conscience laundering' – feeling better about accumulating more than any one person could possibly need to live on by sprinkling a little around as an act of charity … But this just keeps the existing structure of inequality in place. The rich sleep better at night, while others get just enough to keep the pot from boiling over. Nearly every time someone feels better by doing good, on the other side of the world (or street), someone else is further locked into a system that will not allow the true flourishing of his or her nature or the opportunity to live a joyful and fulfilled life. (Buffett 2013)

Arguably, some good has come from these philanthropic actors (e.g. mass health and education programs). However, they seldom challenge the structures facilitating the accumulation of wealth and inequalities. Philanthropy has long been critiqued as a feel-good activity for the rich that allows them to appear altruistic without diminishing their wealth. These concerns over the relationship between benevolent donors and representations of the poor, poverty, and inequality are even more critical now that Western charity campaigns promulgate such discourses.

Western public and popular representations of development

Since the 1980s, a vast proliferation of campaigns, charity adverts, musical movements, fair trade marketing crusades, celebrity endorsements, and media promotions to support international development have inundated the Global North. Western publics are now actors and agents of development, gaining their knowledge of poverty, inequality, and other development concerns from very public representations of the lives, needs, vulnerabilities, and aspirations of people in distant places. This wider, more popular dimension of the Western development industry has initiated discussions around global social responsibility and the ethics of care articulated through notions of a common humanity.

Visual images have become increasingly indispensable to these campaigns. Distant people principally come to understand their relations with each other through visual iconography (Lambert 2010; Mitchell 1987). Indeed, we are at a critical juncture for visualisation. Screens proliferate and social media users are migrating away from text-based platforms (e.g. Twitter) to image-dominated platforms such as Instagram (Ibrahim 2015). However, cultures of visualisation are at best superficial and at worst damaging to the prospects of shared global recognition since distant others are reduced to spectacles and commodities (not people to engage with and recognise; Silverstone 2006). The inclusion of Western 'general publics' in development has further reified borders and boundaries between donor and recipient, West and the rest, rich and poor, as well as distinctions based on 'race' and gender.

Chouliaraki (2013) suggests that the problem is not visualisation *per se*, but the fact that visualisation is tainted by commoditisation, neoliberalism, and neo-colonialism. This commodification exists in the context of ethical consumption which, as Abrahamsen (2012: 141) writes, perpetuates 'the idea of Africa ... as a commodity, its poverty and illness symbolic goods in a global economy of signification that allows (predominantly) Western consumers not only to express their identity, but also to reproduce social hierarchies'. Audiences view such imagery through the corrupted culture of narcissism or solipsism that increasingly characterises Western publics (Chouliaraki 2013).

Advertising, media, and campaigns reflect complex relationships between context-specific and ideological images, practices, and uses. For example, photographs of famine victims appropriate suffering and are affective, not simply illustrative. They are designed to emotionally appeal to viewers, not offer a description of some person or place. The images convey that someone is suffering and that we should be sympathetic to their plight and moved to do something (Campbell 2011). However, without context, most viewers are likely to believe that action to alleviate suffering will only come from outside, especially when Indigenous social structures and local actors are erased from the images. The victim is portrayed passively, devoid of agency and history, their suffering appropriated by the lens. Such imagery of the isolated victim awaiting external assistance reinforces colonial relations of power (Campbell 2011). The process of dehumanising and creating difference and distance between 'us' and 'them' further reifies simplistic and unhelpful binaries.

Vulnerable people's appearance in media and visual imagery raises important ethical and political questions about the kinds of affective responses they elicit and seek. These include a range of emotive responses – to care or not and in what ways; to ignore, pity, cry, protest, donate; to feel compassion, sympathy, curiosity, solidarity, revulsion, or even titillation (Boltanski 1999; Chouliaraki 2013; Halttunen 1995). Yet, we must not be tempted to promote equally simplistic 'positive' images that depict children smiling (not crying) or romanticised images of Indigenous people. As Crush (1995: 335) warns, it is 'easier to view the process of de-colonization purely as the subversion of all Western forms of representation, than to suggest what a de-colonized knowledge might actually look like'. Campbell (2011: 84, emphasis in original) reminds us, 'the problem lies with *the absence* of alternatives as much as it does with *the presence* of the stereotypes'.

Shifting the borders: the rising powers and South–South cooperation

Since the early 2000s, the spatial geographies of capitalist development began to shift with the growing visibility and involvement of non-Western development actors. New global economic, social, and political relations emerged through the soaring economic growth and increasing geopolitical influence of the so-called rising powers – Brazil, India, China, and South Africa (BICS). These major players helped drive the expansion and deepening power and reach of South–South cooperation (Russia, an original BRICS, falls beyond the scope of this discussion).

Importantly, this gave 'impetus to increasing debate and consideration of the potentialities (and pitfalls) of a new phase of challenge or construction of alternatives to the hegemonic and neo-colonial politics of the Global North' (Gray and Gills 2016: 558). While the involvement of these Southern actors did not signify a wholesale decline of the West and the rise of the rest, it did materially and imaginatively challenge Western dominance in providing development assistance and arbitrating development knowledge, ideas, and dreams. Given the dynamism and diversity of the Global South, this 'increasingly polycentric development landscape' (Mawdsley 2018: 182) 'ruffles commonly accepted spatialities' (Raghuram et al. 2014: 120). In particular, China's efforts were 'heralded by some as a new era of South–South cooperation', with the Belt and Road Initiative representing the 'most visible embodiment of China's assertive international role' (Mohan 2021: 54).

The BICS became influential drivers of the global economy by providing 'very substantial investments in roads, ports, information and communications technologies and energy production and transmission; as well as minerals/oil, agricultural and manufacturing investment; and stimulating trade and market-building' (Mawdsley 2018: 179). These rising powers are reconfiguring global development, international trade, labour conditions, environmental impacts (Nadvi 2014), energy transitions (Power et al. 2016), diplomacy (McConnell and Woon 2021), and global governance (Gray and Murphy 2013; Larson 2018). While the BICS share some common features, it is important to remember that they are not homogeneous and represent 'nuanced maps' of development (Sidaway 2012: 56).

The economic surge of the BICS and increasing South–South cooperation have created a more heterogeneous global development environment. For Gray and Gills (2016: 557), this reflects 'a vision of mutual benefit and solidarity among the disadvantaged of the world system' and conveys 'the hope that development may be achieved by the poor themselves through their mutual assistance to one another, and the whole world order transformed to reflect their mutual interests vis-à-vis the dominant Global North'. These aspirations are not wholly new, as Global South populations and governments have long reacted to neo-imperial interference (albeit with varying degrees of success). The New International Economic Order and the Non-Aligned Movement provide potent examples. The Non-Aligned Movement was born at the Asia–Africa Conference held in Bandung, Indonesia, in April 1955. The meeting was convened to bring together the leaders of 29 states, largely former colonies in Africa and Asia, to discuss common concerns about resisting the pressures of the major global and former colonial powers, maintaining their independence, and developing joint policies in international relations. Indian President Nehru, a senior statesman, led the conference alongside Indonesian President Sukarno and Egyptian President Nasser. Crucially, the members advocated neutrality, despite the growing polarisation from the ominous emergence of the Cold War and hoped to sidestep the looming influence of both the US and the Soviet Bloc. These newly independent states of the Global South adopted principles of peaceful co-existence and stressed the importance of economic and cultural coop-

eration and human rights. Although the Non-Aligned Movement represented a serious challenge to Western-dominated political and economic
systems in the 1950s and '60s, it waned in subsequent years. However,
the revival of South–South cooperation in the early 2000s was framed
by similar claims to 'shared colonial and postcolonial experiences and
anchored within a wider framework of promoting the collective strength
of the "South"' (Mawdsley 2020: 227).

The economic growth and political confidence of the BICS led to
some amount of de-Westernisation (Mignolo 2018), and solidarity
underpinned some aspects of South–South cooperation (Gray and Gills
2016). To some extent, this 'southernisation of development' did rupture
the 'formerly dominant North–South axis of power and knowledge'
(Mawdsley 2018: 172). They de-centred the historical assumptions that
shaped North–South development geographies by providing alternative
principles of 'development' (Mawdsley 2018: 176). Indeed, the practices
and engagement of the emerging economies with the Global South exist
alongside rapidly shifting 'traditional' aid discourses and development
cooperation. 'Collectively, they are providers of a growing share of
development finance and resources, of distinctive ideas and approaches,
and their presence is increasingly necessary to the credibility and legiti-
macy of older and newer donor forums and development organisations'
(Mawdsley 2018: 174).

While these paradigmatic shifts and an increasingly multipolar world
have caused considerable concern among 'traditional' development actors
(Li et al. 2021), the North–South axis of global development has largely
persisted. As Zarakol (2019: 214) contends, 'the "Rise of the Rest" is – paradoxically – both hype and reality, both fiction and fact'. The West's interest in 'rising powers' has little to do with actual structural shifts in favour
of 'the Rest' and more to do with Western anxieties about global finance,
security, and foreign policy. Moreover, South–South cooperation does
not fundamentally shift longstanding colonial relations, assumptions, and
representations. Additionally, the arrangement of contemporary South–
South cooperation differs significantly from earlier periods characterised
by the Non-Aligned Movement. Today, South–South partnerships are
largely focused on promoting '(supposedly) mutually beneficial economic
growth as the primary engine of "development"' (Mawdsley 2018: 179),
not directly resisting neo-colonialism or neoliberal exploitation. Thus,
while the 'locus of development (studies) may have shifted away from

a North–South axis to more diffuse and complex relations of connectedness, these relations continue to be racialised, power-laden, and inexorably linked to the development of capitalism' (Mohan 2021: 71). Modes of capitalist development prevail, even in this multipolar world. They are now promoted by both Global North and Global South partners, elites, and governments.

The increasing diversity of development actors blurs spatial demarcations dividing developed and underdeveloped regions of the world. Bordering practices are, in various ways, being transgressed, and the conceptual and geographical boundaries of development are now more fluid, dynamic, and contested. Borders are continuously being made and unmade: we now find instances of the 'Global South in the North', which refers to the increasing relative poverty among populations in the Global North and the role of diasporas in shaping the field of development. Some changes in the spatial bordering of development have not fundamentally altered the hegemony of economic growth in development (e.g. the growing role of the BICS). However, other shifts have forged a space for alternative narratives to emerge. The next chapter illustrates how feminist, postcolonial, and decolonial analyses (among others) have opened the field and allowed the voices of those previously marginalised to be heard. These changes have occurred alongside growing global public action and activism asserting notions of global humanity, solidarity, and responsibility, issues we return to later.

4 Critically (re)thinking development

In the previous chapters, we outlined some of the problematic histories, approaches, and practices of development. This chapter moves on to consider theories and perspectives that decentre and reconstruct those more orthodox approaches. We identify critical discourses that challenge the meaning of development and advance new, more radical directions. These include postcolonialism and decoloniality, post-development, critical understandings of accumulation and dispossession, feminisms and intersectionality, and Indigenous knowledge. While no single narrative can capture the field, together these multiple and diverse perspectives challenge how development is conceived, theorised, and practised. They do not tinker around the edges of development to address this or that problem; rather, they have the potential to reframe the whole conversation.

The political, social, and environmental landscape of developing countries and their global relations continue to be informed by the colonial legacy. Yet, the post-World War II period also brought about profound shifts with challenges to conceptions of modernisation and progress. These revealed how modernisation can only be achieved through exploitation, dispossession, and the denial of plurality. Modernisation ultimately celebrates itself as the desired state of humanity at the expense of the rest of the world (Brohman 1995; Mignolo 2011). It has a profound impact on Global South subjectivities. The inherent implications of backwardness and parochialism attributed to non-Western societies become further entrenched when 'progress' is used to describe a change from a position of deficit or inferiority to one of advancement, improvement, or maturity (Burman 2007: 225). As Sachs (2010: 10, emphasis in original) notes, for many people of the so-called Third World, the 'meaning of "development" is a *reminder of what they are not*. It is a reminder of an undesirable, undignified state. To escape from it, they need to be enslaved to others' experiences and dreams'.

Critical interrogations of the ideas underpinning development, 'alternative' approaches to development, and analyses of the language of development gained momentum from the 1980s (see Ferguson 1990; Sachs 1992). This work sought to reveal the many tenacious strands of colonial forms of knowing and representing embedded in development. For example, Crush (1995) and Escobar (1995) illustrated how development ideology is produced and reproduced in ways that valorise particular forms of (Western) knowledge and maintain the economic and intellectual superiority of the West.

Escobar examined the professionalisation of development knowledge and the institutionalisation of development practices to argue against grand alternative models or strategies. Instead, he advocates a move towards investigating 'alternative representations and practices in concrete local settings, particularly as they exist in contexts of hybridisation, collective action and political mobilisation' (Escobar 1995, 19). Others focused on critiquing the Eurocentrism of much development theory (Hettne 1995; Mabogunje 1989). Mehmet's book *Westernising the Third World* (1995) provides an instructive example. He surveys neo-classical development paradigms to highlight the Eurocentrism of economic development theories and raise concerns about the adverse effects of what he calls Western developmentalism.

In the following sections, we introduce some of the most prominent critiques of mainstream development. These critical approaches have informed an ongoing rethinking of development, despite being long marginalised. For ease of presentation, each theory is summarised separately here; however, in reality, they are not distinct and clearly bounded theories but thoroughly interconnected and dynamic, ceaselessly reworked and evolving.

Postcolonial critiques

Postcolonial approaches emerged to illuminate and resist the ways in which the West produces knowledge about other people in other places and to reveal how contemporary global inequalities are shaped, in part, by ongoing colonial power relations. Specifically, postcolonialism challenges the power of development to crudely ascribe particular characteristics, such as less developed or backward, onto different societies. Thus, while 'finding useful intersections of development studies and postcolonial studies can be a challenge' (Sylvester 2006: 66), it is important and fruitful when rethinking development.

While the idea of 'postcolonialism' has long been debated (see Ahmad 1995; Bhabha 1984; Hall 1997; McClintock 1995; Shohat 1992), 'postcolonial theory' most often serves as an umbrella term for diverse critical approaches that deconstruct Anglo-European thought. Since the early 1990s, postcolonial critiques have emerged to problematise development and the construction of Western knowledge and intellectual traditions. These critiques are deeply suspicious of the totalising theories, grand projects, and truth claims of enlightenment thinking that reinscribed the non-West into a history beyond its own making (Pieterse and Parekh 1995).

The 'post' in postcolonialism does not merely refer to the historical period following the independence of former colonies (as if there is a clear distinction between the 'before' of colonialism and the 'after' of independence). Such an interpretation conceals how history unfolds and obscures the colonial legacy of present-day inequalities. Rather, the 'post' implies a critical engagement 'beyond' colonialism. It signifies changes in power structures while acknowledging the persistence of colonial forms of political, economic, and cultural power and knowledge. It denotes a wholesale critique of Western structures of knowledge and power (McClintock 1994) or, as Young (1990) suggests, a critique of history. Bhabha similarly reminds us of the centrality of representations, 'the term postcolonial is increasingly used to describe that form of social criticism that bears witness to those unequal and uneven processes of representation by which the historical experience of the once-colonised Third World comes to be framed in the West' (Bhabha, quoted in Mongia 1996: 1). To understand the relationship between colonialism and development, postcolonialism 'produces new ways of thinking' that challenge the universalism of Eurocentric theories' (Raghuram and Madge 2006: 270). Specifically, dominant, normalised ideologies around, for example, individual freedom, democracy, rule of law, property, and gender are framed as a product of a particular time and place, emerging from a particular socio-cultural or political context.

The central tenets of postcolonial analysis include identifying the ongoing legacy of colonialism in the present and bringing to the fore the neglected histories and stories of marginalised figures to offer alternative narratives. As such, postcolonialism aims to problematise, deconstruct, and decentre the supposed universality of Western knowledge. Postcolonial approaches demand that scholars rethink the ontological and epistemological positioning of their research and practices. This includes acknowledging and challenging how sites of knowledge production and circulation, and so-called development expertise, are associated with universities, governments, and institutions in and of the Global North, specifically the US and the UK.

While postcolonial approaches have instigated many advances in development thinking and methods, much development practice continues to reproduce colonial representations. This is, in part, because of the dehumanising representations detailed in the previous chapter.

Feminisms and intersectionality

Feminisms and women's movements have long informed global and national politics and protests, including, for example, anti-colonial campaigns for independence and demands for universal suffrage. However, feminist thinking only began to seriously inform development approaches, policies, and practices from the 1970s. Liberal feminism dominated the 1970s: there was growing awareness that development processes were highly gendered, impacting men and women differently, with women consistently losing out. As Harding (2016: 1072) reminds us, 'modernization and its development theories, policies, and practices ... have always been masculinized'. As such, any advantages from development interventions were bypassing women because of ideological, conceptual, and methodological assumptions. Indeed, women were largely invisible to development planners and, therefore, development had adverse effects on women's lives.

Until the 1970s, mainstream research, policy, and planning virtually ignored women's economic roles. It stereotypically assumed that women's activities were confined to the non-economic sphere of reproduction. Subsequently, Women in Development became a major policy concern and many development agencies committed to making visible the full extent of women's economic participation and women's status in terms of income, health, and education. In 1975, the UN's Decade for Women prioritised disaggregating all national economic and social statistics by sex and developing policy approaches that focused on equity and women's empowerment. Subsequently, Gender and Development (GAD) approaches emerged, which did not focus on women *per se*, but on the socially constructed relations between men and women (see Pearson 2005). GAD became increasingly important within development theory and practice. Indeed, teaching GAD is a mode of intervention into a particular hegemonic development narrative (Mohanty 1991) that demands the re-examination of the development process (see Elson 1995; Kabeer 1994, 2012). These approaches exposed gender disparities in, for example, land ownership, employment, access to education, and political participation. They also acknowledged the impacts of unequal gendered divisions of labour that excluded women from certain economic activities (since women were primarily responsible for undertaking social reproduction tasks within and beyond the home).

However, as these approaches were mainstreamed into the agendas of the World Bank and other large development agencies, they tended to lose their radical edge; feminist discourses were often co-opted and depoliticised. Development effectively deradicalised the critical feminist discourses that made unequal relations of power visible. Furthermore, these approaches could not account for the multiple and varied ways that people (men and women) were differently positioned in society based on other factors such as class, sexuality, race, and stage in life cycle. Therefore, critical feminist approaches began foregrounding intersectionality and the plurality of feminisms (and patriarchies), shaping lives and politics in the Global South and North.

This acknowledgement of diverse histories and ontologies countered development interventions that had previously reduced heterogeneity and diversity to create a singular, composite 'Third World Woman'. As Kapur (2002: 37) writes, this

> category is disempowering and does not translate into an emancipatory politics. It produces the fiction of a universal sisterhood, bonded in its experience of victimization and violence. There is no space in this construction for difference or for the articulation of a subject that is empowered. Indeed, the victim subject collapses easily into Victorian/colonial assumptions of women as weak, vulnerable, and helpless. It also feeds into conservative, right-wing agendas for women, which are protectionist rather than liberating. Additionally, it encourages states to resort to the criminal law to address women's rights issues, an arena of law in which nation-states enjoy the powers of moral surveillance and regulation.

Chandra Mohanty's (1984) critical work argued that representations of what she called 'Third World Difference' oppressed most, if not all, women in Global South countries. It reductively assumes that women are victimised always and everywhere, unrelentingly oppressed by *their* cultures. Through this production of 'Third World Difference', 'Western feminisms appropriate and "colonize" the fundamental complexities and conflicts which characterize the lives of women of different classes, religions, cultures, races, and castes in these countries' (Mohanty 1984: 335). The dehumanisation of the subaltern woman depicts her as ignorant, poor, uneducated, tradition-bound, domestic, family-orientated, and victimised (Mohanty 1984). The stereotypical and singular 'Third World Woman' was positioned opposite the Western woman who, by default, was represented as educated, modern, and in control of her body and life.

Mohanty and other postcolonial feminists have long noted the problematic nature of feminisms that elevate gender as the 'primary axis of power[; instead, we must] insist ... on the salience of race, class, sexuality, and nationality, along with gender, in shaping the lives of women' (Thobani 2005: 221). These scholars argue for intersectionality, a framework with roots in diverse intellectual traditions, including Black feminist thought and Third World feminism. An early use of intersectional frameworks was the 'Combahee River Collective Statement' released in 1982 by a grassroots feminist initiative of Boston-based African American women. This important declaration outlined the limits of race-only or gender-only frameworks in analysing the social injustices that shape African American women's lives. Broadly, intersectionality denotes 'the critical insight that race, class, gender, sexuality, ethnicity, nation, ability, and age operate not as unitary, mutually exclusive entities, but as reciprocally constructing phenomena that in turn shape complex social inequalities' (Collins 2015: 2).

As May (2015: 6) suggests, this approach allows for consideration of historical injustices to: 'imagine future possibilities and reconsider omissions, past and present, from a "matrix" mindset ... [it] also helps to expose historical silences and to understand oppression and privilege as lived experiences and processes situated in and shaped by material, political, and social conditions'. These early formulations continue to influence recent debates on intersectionality within development. The intersectional approach is particularly influential in work on migration that attends 'to the multiple social structures and inequalities that interact to shape the specific positions and identities of migrants' (Gao and Hopkins 2022: 177; see also Anthias 2012; Bastia 2014).

Despite the widespread (and growing) adoption of intersectional approaches, Collins warns that intersectionality-as-praxis and the doing of social justice work are often overlooked. Intersectionality is not just 'a field of study to be mastered or an analytical strategy for understanding' (Collins 2015: 16). Rather, its demands for social justice are situated within and across relations of power. This complexity cannot be reduced to singular categories. Therefore, as Anthias (2013: 3) writes, intersectional approaches will continue to provide a 'corrective to essentialising identity constructs that homogenise social categories'.

Accumulation through dispossession and expulsion

In Chapter 2, we explained how conventional ideas of development generally position economic development as a system of exchange. However, this approach fundamentally overlooks critiques of capitalism as the dominant global economic system. Such understandings are essential in illuminating why hierarchies and inequalities are reproduced by economic development. Development goals of economic growth and equity are often incompatible since wealth accumulation relies on the exploitation of labour and unequal access to resources.

At a very basic level, we can understand capitalism as an economic system centred around private ownership and control over the means of production (e.g. resources, tools, equipment, and technology). Capitalism is a social relationship between those who own and control the means of production and those who produce goods and services in exchange for a payment or wage. Wealth is accumulated by profiting off the sales of the goods and services produced by the workers (or, increasingly, by machines). Some of these profits are then reinvested to generate yet more profit. Capitalist processes exploit and expropriate by keeping production costs low, using cheap resources and cheap labour, and/or gaining higher market prices. Labour and resources may be expropriated through, for example, slavery, colonisation, and accumulation by dispossession.

David Harvey (2003) coined the term accumulation by dispossession to explain how contemporary globalised capitalism dispossesses people and places of their resources. This includes new forms of dispossession by financialisation,

> such as credit fraud, speculation, and debt-based financing to the Global South from the Global North, as well as by new methods of enclosing of the global commons, such as the patenting of seeds and genetic material in the name of intellectual property rights, the degradation of the environment, and the privatization of previously public goods such as water, utilities, and universities. (Harvey 2003: 147–8)

These tactics ensure that wealth is increasingly concentrated (Piketty 2017). Accumulation by dispossession has left many people without the means to survive, let alone secure the promise of a living wage. As Chatterjee (2008: 55) explains, 'large sections of peasants who are today the victims of the primitive accumulation of capital are completely unlikely to be absorbed into the new capitalist sectors of growth'. The processes of contemporary expropriation are integral to the inner workings of capitalism. They also operate along racialised and gendered lines. Feminist scholars and those who critique racial capitalism show how race and gender are organising grammars that dehumanise populations. They render some bodies available for exploitation while other, often white, bodies are protected by human rights (Bhattacharyya 2018; Robinson 2000).

Saskia Sassen (2014) suggests that contemporary dislocations and dispossession cannot be explained solely through conventional understandings of expropriation, poverty, and injustice. She suggests they are better understood as *expulsions* of people from a sustainable society. Sassen offers four processes through which these expulsions take place. The first is increasing unemployment from structural adjustment programs and ever-shrinking economies. Second, she argues that land grabs, especially in Africa, result in people being expelled from their own land and places of work. The third process she identifies is the increasing financialisation that caused so many people to lose their homes, and the fourth is global environmental destruction and degradation. The theory of expulsions lays 'bare the extent to which the sheer complexity of the global economy makes it hard to trace lines of responsibility for the displacements, evictions, and eradications it produces – and equally hard for those who benefit from the system to feel responsible for its depredations' (Sassen 2014: 9). Accumulation through dispossession and expulsion provide a useful theoretical and empirical lens to better understand new ways in which poverty and inequality are sustained.

Post-development

Post-development emerged in the 1980s to critique development discourses and practices and the hegemonic principles organising social life (Esteva and Escobar 2017). Post-development scholars and activists questioned why diverse societies were measured according to Western models of progress which centred individualised subjects and capitalist processes. These measures classified many populations and non-capitalist practices as subordinate and inferior (Klein and Morreo 2019). They also overlooked the side of modernity in which colonisation, accumulation by dispossession, and exploitation had been integral (Mignolo 2011). Post-development scholars further identified how development discourse strongly privileged European and Anglo-American expertise and technology, effectively obscuring coloniality, patriarchy, and other power relations (Escobar 1995; Ziai 2007). They argued that Western prescriptions overlooked and marginalised 'pluriversality', diverse ontologies, and ecologies of knowledge, rendering them 'traditional' and essentially non-credible.

Post-development approaches sought to displace the universalisation and globalisation of modernity. They insisted on what Esteva, paraphrasing the Zapatista motto, described as 'a world in which many worlds can be embraced' (Esteva and Escobar 2017: 4). As Colombian scholar Arturo

Escobar (1995: 215), a major post-development thinker, wrote over three decades ago, '[w]e are not looking for development alternatives but alternatives to development'. For Escobar, post-development entails a set of key principles: support for pluralistic grassroots movements, tempering localised relations of power, and upholding a critical stance on established scientific discourses and development expertise refracted through the postcolonial state. Post-development promotes different conceptions of the economy that account for solidarity and align with other schools of thought, such as degrowth, to promote different forms of valuation (Klein and Morreo, 2019).

Some critique post-development for its supposed romanticisation of local alternatives and traditions. However, Escobar (1995: 170) and others caution against both embracing localism 'uncritically as alternatives; or to dismiss [it] as romantic expositions'. Post-development scholars are also criticised for not providing any concrete alternatives to development; however, they argue that post-development is already well underway in practice. In countless urban and rural communities in the South, especially in grassroots organisations and self-help movements, new social structures are being created in reaction to the failure of 'development' (Demaria and Kothari 2017). These alternatives are based on reclaiming the economy from the market, reclaiming politics from the state, and reclaiming knowledge from science. Such processes enable the formation of the 'pluriverse', a critically important idea we return to in Chapter 8.

Indigenous knowledges and ontologies

Development Studies and other disciplines in the social sciences and humanities have long neglected and silenced Indigenous knowledges. Indeed, much literature within the social sciences on the construction and articulation of knowledge is deeply rooted in a Western mindset that marginalises other knowledges (Barker et al. 1994; Crush 1995; Moore-Gilbert 1997; Said 1979; Shohat and Stam 1994). Much writing and research in Development Studies has overtly or indirectly rendered Indigenous knowledges inferior, despite research being 'a process that exploits Indigenous peoples, their culture, their knowledge, and their resources' (Smith 1999: 24). 'Too often, Western scientists re-enact the extractive nature of colonialism by asserting dominant Western positivistic approaches over different worldviews, by writing on behalf of Indigenous communities, or by attempting to interpret Indigenous knowledge and practices' (Caretta and Morgan 2021: 762; see also Ford et al. 2016). Dominant research is a deeply extractive practice; thus, to avoid reproducing a different coloniality, Tynan (2021) calls on non-Indigenous scholars to be attentive to how histories and stories are understood and shared. Okri (2015: 112) affirms this, saying, 'anything that affects our perception of the world usually comes in the form of a story. So, we must be aware of the stories that we imbibe'.

Early attempts to recognise the importance of Indigenous knowledge focused on what was referred to as 'local knowledge'. These efforts often utilised participatory approaches to development, specifically the tools and techniques of Participatory Rural Appraisal (see Chambers 1992, 1997; Oakley 1991). Broadly,

> the aim of participatory development is to increase the involvement of socially and economically marginalised people in decision-making over their own lives. The assumption is that participatory approaches empower local people with the skills and confidence to analyse their situation, reach consensus, make decisions and take action, so as to improve their circumstances. The ultimate goal is more equitable and sustainable development. (Guijt and Shah 1998: 1)

While this alternative approach to development encouraged 'learning reversals', critics argued that participatory approaches became yet another authoritative discourse to further conceal the agency of the 'outsider' or 'expert' and reinforce unequal power relations (Cooke and Kothari 2001). Indigenous knowledges go beyond participatory approaches and 'local knowledge'; they fundamentally challenge the ontological orientation of Western thought (Viveiros de Castro 2013),

> not in the different perspectives each may take upon the world (their respective 'world-views' or even 'cultures'), but rather in the ways in which either of them may come to define what may count as a world, along with its various constituents, in the first place … the difference pertains to the ontological question of what things *are* or indeed *could be*, rather than how they might be differentially 'represented', 'known' (or at least 'believed'), or for that matter, 'constructed'. (Holbraad 2013: 470)

This 'ontological turn' highlights how certain differences cannot simply be 'encompassed and captured by one's own symbolic, cultural, or political apparatus'. 'Some differences are the product of different realities rather than different subjective takes on reality' (Hage 2012: 302).

Indigenous knowledges are embedded in social institutions (Naess 2013), particular places, relationships, and practices (Muir et al. 2010). They often draw on holistic frameworks that bring together natural and spiritual worldviews (Boillat and Berkes 2013; Cochran et al. 2014). While there has been a push to integrate Indigenous knowledges into formal academic assessments (see Intergovernmental Science-Policy Platform on Biodiversity and Ecosystem Services; Tengö et al. 2014; Tengö et al. 2017), most Western science continues to devalue Indigenous knowledges and fails to recognise their centrality to the ongoing process of contesting and rethinking development.

Decolonisation and decoloniality

Recent global protests for transformative and structural change and calls to decolonise knowledge have catalysed a rethinking of how historical colonialist narratives persist in the present. These include 'Rhodes Must Fall' and related campaigns demanding the decolonisation of public spaces and histories (Mpofu and Ndlovu-Gatsheni 2019), global movements against racism and injustice such as Black Lives Matter, and the insistence within parts of academia that Indigenous knowledges and forms of knowing be recognised. Together, they present significant challenges for the field of development. This critical moment is replete with potential and necessitates new forms of decolonial writing that recognise how colonial forms of knowledge are not relegated to the past but persist in the present. As Noxolo (2017: 342) writes,

> decolonial writing must emerge from a different positionality. Classically, its scholars are Indigenous, or First Nations people, and there is nothing 'former' or 'post' about the colonialism that they write about: they are writing out of and about the continuous colonisation and re- (or neo-) colonisation of the countries where their ancestors have always lived.

These calls for critical scholarship echo Edward Said's (1981: 164) insight that, 'underlying every interpretation of other cultures is the choice facing the individual scholar or intellectual; whether to put intellect at the service of power or at the service of criticism, communities, and moral sense'.

Such conversations have long taken place within academic literature (e.g. wa Thiong'o's *Decolonising the Mind*, 1986) and in fiction (e.g. Chinua Achebe's *Things Fall Apart*, 1958). Despite these provocative texts and postcolonial and feminist critiques, the coloniality of development has not been significantly altered – old distinctions and hierarchies between people, places, and knowledge persist. While the project of decolonising development is implicitly addressed through writings on race, racism, and development (Kothari 2006a; Shilliam 2014), decolonial analytical lenses that assess hierarchies of knowledge are largely absent. Yet, the project of decolonising development is currently enjoying a revival. While such discussions are in their infancy (Patel 2020), they still offer critical understandings into how historically based assumptions, colonial roots, and structural contexts continue to influence the field of development. For example, the resignation of many of *Third World Quarterly*'s editorial board members in 2017 after the journal published an article making the case for colonialism reminds us that the project of decolonising academia remains an urgent imperative.

Decolonial approaches ask who is allowed to produce ideas and theories and what counts as scholarly knowledge. The inclusion of Indigenous and non-Western perspectives encourages a rethinking of the world from the margins (of academia), an imperative in producing greater epistemic diversity. Thus, the growing decolonial scholarship builds on, and goes beyond, postcolonialism.

However, transforming principles into actual practice is challenging. In their 2018 text, *On Decoloniality*, Mignolo and Walsh reflect on the problems involved in achieving this transformation, given the depth of coloniality's pervasive effects. Robinson (2000: 243) writes, 'if another world is possible, it cannot be built with the conceptual tools inherited from the renaissance and the enlightenment'. And, as Audre Lorde (1983: 96) put it, 'the master's tools will never dismantle the master's house'. Others suggest that decolonial thought should transcend, not dismantle, Western ideas. Following Lorde's metaphor, Gordon and Gordon (2015) advocate building new houses and, when enough are built, the hegemony of the master's house – in fact, mastery itself – will no longer sustain its imperial status.

Decoloniality requires a fundamental shift away from the language, knowledge, and aims of non-Indigenous or Western researchers and toward the agendas of Indigenous people and people from the Global South. As Indigenous scholars explain, decoloniality allows Indigenous people to make sense of their own reality rather than having non-Indigenous peoples and societies define it for them. However, as Grosfoguel writes, decolonising knowledge also entails moving away from the postcolonial provincialising of Western claims. Rather than integrating Indigenous thought into pre-existing frameworks, the decolonial turn encourages a rethinking of the world *from* Latin America, *from* Africa, *from* Indigenous places, and so on (Grosfoguel 2011; see also Comaroff and Comaroff 2012).

However, others warn that even if coloniality can be critiqued, disobeyed, defied, and disrupted, it cannot be totally removed or overcome – to assume so ignores its 'hydra-like nature and force' (Walsh 2020: 605). Thus, decoloniality should at least be concerned with introducing a '(m) ore critical understanding of the underlying assumptions, motivations and values that inform research practices … to serve as a reminder, of the need to reflect on, and be critical of, one's own culture, values, assumptions, and beliefs and to recognise these are not the "norm"' (Wilson 2001: 214–7).

Decolonising development must go beyond rhetoric and academic exercises. At a minimum, it requires Western academics to reflect on their own roles and understand how decolonisation sometimes entails giving up space, not being involved, and being silent. It also requires being vigilant about how calls to decolonise can be appropriated. As Noxolo (2017: 2) reminds us, 'decolonial theory can become yet another instrument for time-honoured colonialist manoeuvres of discursively absenting, brutally exploiting, and then completely forgetting Indigenous people'. Esson et al. (2017: 384) astutely articulate these and other concerns:

> this pursuit of critical consciousness via decolonial thinking could do more harm than good … the emphasis on decolonising knowledges rather than structures, institutions and praxis reproduces coloniality, because it recentres non-Indigenous, white and otherwise privileged groups in the global architecture of knowledge production. It is argued that an effective decolonial movement necessitates that the terms on which the discipline starts debates about decolonisation and decoloniality are determined by those racialised as Indigenous and non-white by coloniality.

Furthermore, Tuck and Yang (2012: 2–3) caution,

> Decolonization, which we assert is a distinct project from other civil and human rights-based social justice projects, is far too often subsumed into the directives of these projects, with no regard for how decolonization wants something different than those forms of justice ... Decolonize (a verb) and decolonization (a noun) cannot easily be grafted onto pre-existing discourses/frameworks, even if they are critical, even if they are anti-racist, even if they are justice frameworks.

Tuck and Yang (2012: 3) also reiterate that decolonisation is not a metaphor for 'things we want to do to improve our societies' – it is fundamentally material, about 'the repatriation of Indigenous land and life'. This is a particular challenge to settler societies where colonisation continues and, unless land is given back, 'decolonisation' will remain as simply a metaphor.

Additionally, there are concerns about the ease with which the language of decolonisation has been adopted. The imperative to decolonise development entails remaining continually alert to how decolonising discourses are being articulated and by whom. Rumbukwella (2022: 1), for example, warns that decoloniality is in some instances, 'insufficiently self-reflexive of how its conceptual premises are appropriated by nativist discourses'. In the past, Development Studies has quickly integrated, sanitised, and purified radical discourses and practices. Earlier critical development literature reveals how commonplace it is for these radical discourses to be co-opted into the mainstream and depoliticised: in the 1980s, feminism became GAD; in the 1990s, radical consciousness-raising became participatory development; and in the 2000s, powerful anti-racism theory and activism was transmuted into cultural sensitivity and culture and development.

We may already be witnessing a watering down of the decoloniality concept, as many politically diverse individuals and institutions have adopted its language (e.g. decolonising universities, decolonising the curriculum, decolonising research and knowledge, etc.). Even those who are actively reproducing forms of coloniality now speak of the need to decolonise. Even if decolonising imperatives were to be more substantively deployed, past tendencies to co-opt critical discourses suggest that decoloniality could lose its radical edge. However, this could also be mitigated since, as Esson et al. (2017) remind us, decolonisation makes loud and radical challenges, especially when it is directly linked to protests, global campaigns and movements, and direct confrontations with existing practice. We are positioned at a critical moment when it may be possible to find political, radical, and creative ways to decolonise development. Therefore, we must consider what the decolonial turn means for the future of Development Studies. What would development look like after decolonisation, given its colonial genealogy and lingering colonial legacies? We will return to this fundamental question in the final chapter.

Critical thinking

Postcolonialism, feminisms, post-development, Indigenous knowledges, and decoloniality offer critical insights into (ways of conceiving) development. While this chapter presented each of these ideas separately, they are not distinct nor bounded in practice. For example, postcolonial feminism de-centres Western knowledge while also challenging masculinist knowledge. It reveals the importance of bridging understandings of gender and race when analysing inequality and injustice (see McEwan 2018; McLeod 2020). Early postcolonial feminists such as Spivak (1988, 1993), Mani (1989), Minh-Ha (1987, 1989), hooks (1992, 1994), and Mohanty (1991, 1992) forged theoretical space for a 'postcolonial feminism' that rejected any analytical separation between gender, race, and imperialism. Indeed, the impossibility of discussing colonialism without making connections to gender relations and Indigenous knowledge is now widely recognised (Kothari 1997). Other critical scholars, such as Briggs and Sharp (2004), use postcolonial theory to examine how Indigenous knowledges have been included in the development process. Despite these advances in critical scholarship, the risk of co-optation, mainstreaming, and losing the radical edge, remains a key obstacle to sustaining progressive discourses in development research, policy, and practice. We must ensure that these approaches remain critical, despite the ever-increasing professionalisation of development, which tends to prioritise administrative policy over critical theory (Chouliaraki 2013). We will soon return to the critical ways of thinking presented in this chapter to explore how we might use them in forging new articulations of development.

5 Promises of development: employment, health, and education

Even as development priorities have shifted over time, three pillars – employment, health, and education – have remained central. These pillars invoke promises to achieve more equitable and sustainable futures and draw on human development approaches that challenge economic growth-focused development. While goals centring employment, health, and education are widely prioritised, their specific aims and methods are subject to much debate and disagreement. This means that policies that are, at times, conflictual or unsuitable occasionally lead to disastrous results. Nonetheless, health, education, and employment remain hallmarks of mainstream development planning and policy today. These pillars, which are generally embedded in broader discursive norms of modernisation and improvement, are often applied universally, crowding out other possibilities.

Western norms of progress pervade development programs and interventions. Escobar (1995: 87) argues that these norms establish a

> discursive practice that sets the rules of the game: who can speak, from what points of view, with what authority, and according to what criteria of expertise; it sets the rules that must be followed for this or that problem, theory or object to emerge and be named, analysed and eventually transformed into a policy or plan.

These norms limit the expression of non-Western actors' alternative meanings and obscure the plurality of perspectives about what constitutes meaningful development goals (Olivier de Sardan 2008). These normative ideas and practices are most often disseminated through technical expertise, or what the development industry calls 'technical assistance'. Knowledge transferred in the form of 'technology' is often presented as scientific, impartial, and apolitical (Borda-Rodriguez and Lanfranco 2011). This renders development into a technical problem to be solved through technical fixes (Li 2011) and reinforces the idea that it is neutral, universally applicable, and inherently good (while hiding social complexities and structural inequalities). When development is envisaged as a technical problem in need of a technological solution, Western meanings of development are often privileged, and existing power relations can become further embedded (Olivier de Sardan 2008; Mosse 2004).

The processes to modernise education, health, and employment epitomise this approach. These development goals would appear to require the transfer of technical expertise, usually from aid-giving countries to recipient countries. The three pillars feature prominently in the Sustainable Development Goals (SDGs). However, despite multiple successes in addressing these areas, inequalities and exclusion continue to increase. This chapter illuminates progress made and challenges that persist in achieving these promises of development.

Working for development: employment and labour

One enduring indicator of progress is the presence of an economic system based on wage labour. Waged labour, a contract of payment for work, is a common way for people to obtain economic security. However, researchers have long noted the tensions between political systems valorising waged work and economic systems that do not provide adequate and full employment for all (Standing 2014).

Processes of accumulation dispossess many people from their land and/ or opportunities to make a stable, living wage (Ferguson 2017; Li 2010). Such displacement and expropriation of land and labour compound insecurity. For example, rural communities in India have been dispossessed and displaced from their land by dams and other large infrastructural projects funded by national and international capital in the name of development (D'Costa 2014). While these processes may generate some formal employment, they cannot absorb the large numbers of people dispossessed of their means of survival.

Hickel (2019a) argues that this insecurity is rooted in historical colonial relations. He suggests that, prior to colonisation,

> most people lived in subsistence economies where they enjoyed access to abundant commons – land, water, forests, livestock and robust systems of sharing and reciprocity. They had little if any money, but then they didn't need it in order to live well … This way of life was violently destroyed by colonisers who forced people off the land and into European-owned mines, factories and plantations, where they were paid paltry wages for work they never wanted to do in the first place.

While not wanting to romanticise pre-colonial societies, Hickel points out that processes of dispossession endured by societies of the Global South through colonisation included losing access to land with the promise of waged labour. Munck (2013: 758) agrees that,

> throughout the colonial world, the subaltern classes struggled against the imposition of wage labour by the colonialists. There was nothing liberatory about being torn from traditional communal modes of production to become a 'wage slave'. Narratives of modernisation revolved around the supposed civilising influence of capitalist relations of production whereby waged work was seen as the answer to 'tame the recalcitrant multitudes'.

This history lingers today, as 'work and decency were twinned in the colonial imaginary, and that is why the decent work agenda can be seen as less than liberatory from a Southern perspective' (Munck 2013: 758).

Informal economy and work

Waged labour, a constant promise of development, is rarely realised for most of the world's population who continue to live within endemic economic and labour insecurity. Around the world, many people work in the informal sector, informal economy, informal enterprises, farms, and households (Mosoetsa et al. 2016). This 'informal' sector plays a crucial role for the rest of the economy. It provides relative surplus labour that drives down formal labour costs while also delivering sources of cheap labour, resources, and commodities (Harriss-White 2006). The inherent tension in capitalist development is simple: there cannot be enough secure and dignified employment for all because capitalism needs the informal economy to remain informal. Yet, development policies and interventions tend to frame the informal sector as a stage in the larger transition from the informal to the formal economy, where work is regulated by political and judicial processes to ensure labour standards (Bernards 2017; Mead and Morrisson 2004).

National governments and international agencies often adopt this transition-based understanding of labour conditions in the Global South. For example, the World Bank attempts to promote the transformation of informal labour into formal labour by championing entrepreneurial acumen and skills development. Similarly, the International Labour Organization (ILO) introduced policies to encourage inclusive governance and social protection (Bernards 2017). However, some caution against framing informal workers as 'micro-entrepreneurs' or 'self-employed' because this terminology obscures the immense economic uncertainty and precarity in contexts where people must make a living from limited resources, often under oppressive conditions (Ferguson 2015; Rizzo 2011). Additionally, the entrepreneurial approach and social protection policies severely underestimate the enduring connection between labour insecurity and global capitalism (Standing 2014).

Gendered work

Labour and work are characteristically gendered, with women in the Global South, and increasingly in so-called developed countries (Chen 2012), disproportionately concentrated in informal economic activities such as the agricultural and service sectors (ILO 2016). This is compounded by the gendered division of labour between productive and reproductive work (Folbre 2012; Himmelweit 2007; Waring 1999). A variety of divisions segment the work carried out in any society between, for example, paid and unpaid, formal and informal, skilled and unskilled, and mental and manual. Elson's ground-breaking book, *Male Bias in the Development Process* (1995), illustrates how gender cuts across these and other social divisions to produce women's work and men's work.

Within the gendered division of labour, women often have two or more jobs – paid work from formal or informal employment, and unpaid caring work such as looking after children or elderly relatives. For example, women agricultural workers often carry a double burden, doing most of the domestic work in their households on top of activities related to agricultural production. The gender norms regulating men's and women's roles push women to undertake a larger proportion of unpaid work

(Eyben 2012). Such reproductive labour ensures humanity's continuing existence, as there is no society or even life without 'social reproduction'. Feminist political philosopher Nancy Fraser relays some aspects of this important work: 'birthing and socialising the young, the caring for the old, maintenance of households, building communities and sustaining the shared meanings, affective dispositions and horizons of value that underpin social cooperation' (Fraser 2016: 33).

Importantly, capitalist economies rely, even 'free ride' (Fraser 2016), on this unpaid work. Unpaid social reproductive labour is valued because it is a condition for the reproduction and functioning of societies, but no monetary value is attributed to it. Therefore, this work is treated as 'free', even though the formal economy profits from unpaid domestic and care work (Fraser 2016). There have been some attempts to assign a monetary value to such work. For instance, Woetzel et al. (2015) conservatively estimate that unpaid work contributes US\$10 trillion annually, equivalent to 13 per cent of the global GDP. Some development policies focusing on employment seek to address gendered income inequalities by integrating women into formal employment. However, this strategy can increase a woman's work, as she takes on additional paid employment while continuing with unpaid responsibilities, or burden other women, who must now take on her caring roles.

Specific gender-focused policies can address some of these inequalities in work. However, the gender division of labour remains deeply embedded in assumptions about the kinds of work appropriate for men and women. Gendered norms underpin all social relations between men and women and limit women's choices and opportunities in public and private domains (Agarwal 1997). They are the root of overt and covert, direct and indirect, gender discrimination that adversely affect women's rights (Harcourt 2009). Norms instrumentalising and sexualising women's bodies can lead to a range of discriminatory practices, including harassment, limited reproductive rights, assumptions about employability and ability, and violence (Hughes et al. 2015).

Violence against women and girls is physically, socially, and psychologically harmful; it also constrains a woman's agency and limits her opportunities to become economically empowered. UN Women (2006) found that women who are exposed to intimate partner violence are more likely to be employed in casual and part-time work, and their earnings are 60 per cent lower than women who do not experience such violence (World Bank 2016). Sexual harassment is also a concern in formal and informal workplaces, as women are often denied recourse to justice because the police, judiciary, and workplaces do not give due weight to gender-based violence. However, some evidence suggests that women's economic empowerment through access to paid work does have the potential to increase their negotiating power and help them acquire the economic means to leave abusive relationships (Haneef et al. 2014).

Unpaid labour often goes beyond the affective and material care work of raising the young, caring for the elderly, and maintaining homes. It also includes Indigenous notions of contribution that emphasise ecological care and the building and sustaining of communities and cultures. Despite being essential for all societies and economies to function, these activities and responsibilities are rarely acknowledged in economic measurements and are largely invisible in development policies. The following section explores one way that these different kinds of work are beginning to be valued – cash transfers.

Cash transfers

Direct Cash Transfers (CTs) emerged in the late 1990s in response to the growing realisation that promises of full and fair employment were failing since many people globally had no access to wage labour. This led to the 'creation and expansion of extensive social welfare programs targeting the poor anchored in schemes that directly transfer small amounts of cash to large numbers of low-income people' (Ferguson 2015: 15) and growing advocacy to 'just give money to the poor' (Hanlon et al. 2012). Some CT programs included conditions that recipients meet certain criteria (though unconditional transfers of cash also existed). These 'Conditional Cash Transfer' (CCT) programs aimed to reduce poverty

> by making welfare programs conditional upon the receivers' actions. That is, the government only transfers the money to persons who meet certain criteria. These criteria may include enrolling children into public schools, getting regular check-ups at the doctor's office, receiving vaccinations, or the like. They have been hailed as a way of reducing inequality and helping households break out of a vicious cycle whereby poverty is transmitted from one generation to another. (Fiszbein and Schady 2009: 1)

CCTs target payments to vulnerable groups to support specific development goals, such as girls' access to education or improving maternal health care. Mexico's Oportunidades program and Brazil's Bolsa Familia have been credited with alleviating poverty (De Brauw et al. 2014). However, CCTs' targeted and conditional economic security do not address structural inequalities in the wider economy. They are also criticised for imposing conditions that reinforce integration into capitalist economies (Cannon 2014). Furthermore, conditions can 'undermine the social protection value of the transfers by denying them to those who fail to satisfy the conditions' (Loeser et al. 2021: 1).

Some southern African countries have implemented targeted CTs without conditionalities. For example, 30 per cent of South Africa's population receives either an old-age pension or a child support grant and 12 per cent of Namibians receive child maintenance grants. Botswana and Lesotho also offer old-age pensions and a cash payment for childcare, while Eswatini (formerly Swaziland) provides a universal-aged pension. CTs are increasingly seen as an important form of humanitarian assistance that effectively provides economic security for individuals and families (Austin and Frize 2011; Peppiatt et al. 2001). For example, the United Nations High Commissioner for Refugees (UNHCR) has used CTs for refugee returnees in Central America, Afghanistan, Burundi, and Libya since the 1990s. UNHCR also uses CTs in care and maintenance-type emergency recovery operations in protracted conflict situations and in refugee camps (UNHCR 2012).

In *Give a Man a Fish: Reflections on the New Politics of Distribution*, Ferguson (2015: 13) argues that direct CTs represent a 'quiet revolution' in development practice. They mark a fundamental shift in how development agencies can reduce poverty, especially under conditions of mass unemployment. He suggests that CTs offer opportunities to rethink contemporary capitalism, re-examine the relationship between production and distribution, and develop new forms of political mobilisation. An analytical shift away from production and towards distribution could frame CTs as payment for ordinary people's economic contribution to the generation of capital (not as a gift or charity). Ferguson (2015: 186) positions CTs as a 'rightful share' that can radically redistribute wealth: 'the entire production apparatus must be treated as a single, common inheritance'. The shift from job creation to distribution policy is most evident in calls for basic income.

Decommodifying labour and work: a basic income approach

Delinking economic security from waged labour has the potential to address gender and other inequalities in the labour market and value diverse kinds of work. This idea is embodied in the notion of decommodification that provides workers with the ability to choose to leave the labour market, not be forced out by exclusion or compulsion (Saunders 2017).

Achieving decommodification has become increasingly important in contexts where sufficient and secure employment is not available for all. The Basic Income (BI) approach can potentially push society towards decommodification. The approach is based on the provision of a periodic, unconditional cash payment given to all individuals, without means-testing or work requirements (Basic Income Earth Network n.d.). It exists alongside other universal provisions of public goods and services, such as education, health, and infrastructure. The radical potential of the BI approach relies on it being generous enough to significantly redistribute wealth and provide a feasible exit option from wage labour. Ultimately, it could challenge unequal relations between labour, resource distribution, and economic security. This would be more radical than most poverty alleviation measures and has the potential to redefine what work means and to include all forms of productive and reproductive labour (Fouksman and Klein 2019; Weeks 2011). A BI that provides recipients with a universal, secure, unconditional, and regular economic base could create real freedom from exploitation and rising economic insecurity, and the ability to live a life that people value (Standing 2014; Van Parijs 2006). BI also provides a potential alternative in contexts where wage labour can no longer serve as the main basis of social membership (Ferguson 2015; Standing 2014).

UNICEF and the Self Employed Women's Association (SEWA) undertook a 2011 trial in rural India to assess the efficacy of a Universal Basic Income (UBI). Across eight villages in Madhya Pradesh, 6000 men and women were given 200 rupees, and children were given 100 rupees each month. After 12 months, the impacts were compared to non-UBI villages. The payments supported people in developing capabilities and obtaining resources, as well as encouraging them to more effectively participate in economic, social, and political life (Davala et al. 2015; SEWA 2014). Many women began investing in economic and social activities that increased their own income (and that of their household) by up to 16 per cent. In

BI villages, the proportion of girls with normal weight-for-age increased by 25 per cent compared to only 12 per cent in the control villages (Davala et al. 2015; SEWA 2014). Another two-year trial in Namibia's Otjivero-Omitara village found similar results. Residents below the age of 60 years received an unconditional grant of N$100 per person per month. After two years, poverty had been reduced from 76 per cent to 37 per cent, income-generating activities increased from 44 per cent to 55 per cent, and children's weight-for-age improved, with only 10 per cent being considered underweight (down from 42 per cent previously; Haarmann et al. 2009). A more extensive 12-year BI randomised control trial is currently being undertaken in western Kenya by the development NGO GiveDirectly.

The emancipatory value of BI goes beyond its monetary value. Cash payments alleviate the contrived scarcity of money itself, a cause of chronic indebtedness and impoverishment (Standing 2015). Additionally, BI and CT should not be framed as grants or charity, as this obscures structural inequalities and conceals how redistribution represents a 'rightful share' of accumulated wealth (Ferguson 2015: 186). BI and related ideas continue to circulate within international development agencies and national governments but have yet to be fully adopted. Instead, most development policies continue to focus on employment creation and the informal-to-formal economic transition.

Health and development

The COVID-19 pandemic exposed serious shortcomings in health systems around the world and revealed ongoing inequalities in health care provision. For example, advanced economies stockpiled vaccines for their own citizens as people in low-income countries died without access to vaccinations. These inequities reflect a long history of unequal access to care. Patrick Manson and Ronald Ross, the founders of the field of tropical medicine, identified disease as the principal factor holding back populations in colonised nations and argued for improving imperial health endeavours (Worboys 1976). Manson wrote that tropical medicine 'strikes effectively, at the root of the principal difficulty of most of [our tropical] Colonies – disease. It will encourage and cheapen commercial enterprise. It will conciliate and foster the native' (Manson, cited in

Worboys 1976: 85–6). Medicine was seen as simultaneously beneficial to the health of colonised people and good for sustaining colonial rule. Medical practitioners perpetuated racialised, colonial discourses that distinguished between European diseases that were seen as hygienic in nature and tropical diseases that were seen as parasitic, dangerous, and existing beyond the colonial metropole (Worboys 1976: 88). Farmer et al. (2013) argue that contemporary ideas of global health and the establishment of large-scale eradication programs originated from these foundational differences.

Disease eradication programs

Large international health organisations such as the World Health Organization (WHO) emerged in the first half of the 20th century. To move beyond addressing the health problems in Europe's colonies exclusively through the lens of 'tropical medicine', they adopted more international approaches to health and health care. Yet, they continued to reflect the interests of imperial powers – protecting international commerce and worker productivity (Birn et al. 2009). For example, while standardisation and transregional cooperation were encouraged, little consideration was given to local community involvement or local social and economic contexts. Many of these medical and development institutions aimed to modernise 'traditional' and 'non-Western' health care cultures. They focused on populations, not individuals, and established campaigns targeted at specific diseases rather than fostering a comprehensive state of good health. Consequently, a 'one-size-fits-all' approach was often used. For instance, the Rockefeller Foundation pursued a hookworm elimination campaign across the whole of Latin America in the early 1900s, disregarding evidence from some countries, such as Mexico, where hookworm prevalence was limited (Farmer et al. 2013).

The WHO, established in 1948, is the global agency responsible for international health cooperation. Initially, the WHO's eradication programs employed a 'vertical' or top-down approach that targeted specific diseases such as malaria and smallpox. These campaigns were criticised for only using medical knowledge based in Western science and focusing almost exclusively on technological fixes, with little regard for specific social, political, economic, and cultural factors or local medical knowledge (Cueto 2013). Consequently, these large-scale interventions had mixed results and called dominant models of international health and development into question. This led to the development of more 'horizontal' and collaborative health care approaches and gave rise to the primary health care movement.

Primary health care

The 1978 International Conference on Primary Health Care in Alma-Ata in present-day Kazakhstan was a landmark event for global health. It resulted in a declaration affirming that primary health care was the key to attaining Health for All goals. The participating countries agreed to achieve universal primary health care by 2000. Other key goals included defining appropriate medical and public health tools that could be readily deployed in resource-poor settings, increasing community participation in health care delivery, challenging medical elitism, integrating Western and traditional medical practices, and conceptualising health as a primary avenue for social and economic development (Cueto 2004). However, despite its international support, this vision was flawed. No plan was established to demarcate who would pay for, or implement, this world-wide scale-up of primary health care provision. Furthermore, contemporary global economic shifts were underway that would fundamentally transform the international health agenda (Farmer et al. 2013).

The late 1970s and 1980s were a time of major global economic restructuring. Months after the Alma-Ata Conference, a group of policy makers from wealthy nations reconvened to discuss the future of world health in the context of a resource-restrained environment. The new Selective Primary Health Care plan focused on four interventions: child growth monitoring, oral rehydration therapy, breastfeeding, and immunisations. It aimed to offer low-cost, high-impact international health care that could be easily monitored and measured. While these were certainly important areas of health care, these interventions were also criticised for ignoring the structural problems with health care systems caused by the implementation of structural adjustment programs (Cueto 2004).

Throughout the 1980s and 1990s, the World Bank and the International Monetary Fund (IMF) implemented neoliberal policies with far-reaching impacts on health systems and health care provision. Structural adjustment programmes (SAP) intended to stabilise, liberalise, and privatise health care, which was framed as a commodity (not a right) that could be efficiently allocated by the market. The policies were backed by the

IMF and World Bank's conditional lending practices (Farmer et al. 2013), which compelled borrowing countries to restructure their economies and privatise social services if they were to receive loans. This had devastating impacts on the poorest and most vulnerable people in developing countries, who now had to pay for their health care. By the late 1980s, the negative effects of these programs were becoming clear. In 1987, UNICEF published a report titled 'Adjustment with a Human Face' that documented the harmful consequences of these policies on health systems across the developing world (UNICEF 1987). The report detailed how rising interest rates on debt repayments came at the expense of per capita social spending on health and education. Between 1980 and 1985, social spending decreased by an average of 26 per cent in African countries and by 18 per cent in Latin American countries (Farmer et al. 2013). Consequently, structural adjustment programs eroded publicly financed health services in developing countries and led to the severe deterioration of health systems (Bond and Dor 2003; Fort et al. 2004; Navarro 2002).

The right to health

Many global health systems continue to deal with the inequities caused by SAPs. However, in the 1990s, rights-based approaches to development led to improved global health systems. This was partly motivated by the AIDS epidemic. AIDS was framed as a human rights issue (Tarantola et al. 2006) that required the global community to address broader structural issues to curb the spread of the disease (Mann 1997).

From the mid-1990s, other actors gained influence in the field of international health. Philanthropic organisations, such as the Bill and Melinda Gates Foundation (established in 1994), provided finance for international health research and implementation programs. During this period, public–private partnerships (PPPs) became a central modality of international health care (Buse and Walt 2000). These new influencers provided unprecedented funding, with health development assistance from public and private institutions rising from US$8.65 billion in 1998 to US$21.79 billion in 2007. However, private philanthropists and PPPs retained the business sector's role in devising health policies, leaving the field of international health with inadequate accountability frameworks and donor-driven and technologically oriented priorities (Birn et al. 2009).

Three of the Millennium Development Goals (MDGs) also had an explicit health focus (reducing child mortality, improving maternal health, and combatting HIV/AIDS, malaria, and other diseases). Consequently, very real progress in health and health care provision was made. For example, the WHO (2018) reported that

> the number of deaths of children under 5 years of age fell from 12.7 million in 1990 to 6.3 million in 2013. In developing countries, the percentage of underweight children under 5 years old dropped from 28 per cent in 1990 to 17 per cent in 2013. Globally, new HIV infections declined by 38 per cent between 2001 and 2013. Existing cases of tuberculosis are declining, along with deaths among HIV-negative tuberculosis cases.

Global health

Progress in global health since the 1980s included substantial reductions in child mortality, increases in life expectancy, and the elimination of some communicable diseases. Most places have also seen significant advances in health care provision accessibility and standards. The UN SDGs continue to ensure healthy lives and promote well-being for people of all ages with a focus on noncommunicable diseases, mental health, violence, and universal health coverage. The SDGs reflect a shift from international to global health, emphasising how health inequalities and poor health care access are faced by people across the world, as the COVID-19 pandemic so starkly demonstrated.

The recognition of globalised health concerns is necessary and appropriate; however, some scholars warn that global health discourses could obscure the specific health inequalities faced by poorer countries. The Global North may continue defining and dominating global agendas (MacFarlane et al. 2008; Bozorgmehr 2010). Thus, as MacFarlane et al. (2008: 283) argue,

> If global health is about the improvement of health worldwide, the reduction of disparities, and protection of societies against global threats that disregard national borders, it is essential that academic institutions reach across geographic, cultural, economic, gender, and linguistic boundaries to develop mutual understanding of the scope of global health and to create collaborative education and research programs. One indication of success would be emergence of a new generation of truly global leaders working on a shared and well-defined agenda – and doing so on equal footing.

Yet, most development policies continue to privilege Western notions of health and well-being. Programs rarely embrace the diversity, plurality, causes, and consequences of ill health or acknowledge non-Western medicines. This marginalises local and Indigenous knowledges and health care practices used around the world. Such diverse ontologies have much to offer; however, despite recent efforts to decolonise understandings of well-being, health care rarely takes such approaches seriously.

Education: pedagogy of the oppressed

The provision of education, long a building block of development, is now widely considered a basic human right. Universal primary education was central to the MDGs and remains central in the current SDGs. Education is seen as the foundation for social and economic progress since improved education is linked to better health and nutrition, more efficient and effective institutions, and good governance and democracy. For many, educational opportunities promise upward mobility and poverty alleviation. Yet, to understand why education plays such a prominent role, we must determine what is meant by 'education', what constitutes knowledge, and what information is being taught and learned. While education can address inequalities, it can also reinforce relations of power and control. 'Education' means many different things to different people. While it is often portrayed as a process of knowledge generation that can 'free' the mind to think critically, it can also serve wider processes of acculturation such as the transfer of knowledge to assimilate people and reproduce specific norms, ideologies, and ways of thinking.

During colonial times, Christian missionaries often used education to control and assimilate people into European Enlightenment ideology. Missionary education was a form of soft power to convert people to European Christian values, often with the promise of food, shelter, and protection. Missionaries presented themselves as the 'saints of civilisation', while those who rejected their teachings were portrayed as 'savages and barbarians'. Christian education specifically targeted customary belief systems and offered to save people from themselves. It also justified continued colonial expansion and softened resistance through assimilation and coercion. As Thomas Macaulay, the architect of colonial Britain's educational policy in India, famously declared, 'we must do our best to form a class … of persons Indian in blood and colour, but English in taste, in opinions, words and intellect' (Macaulay, quoted in Hall 2009: 787). Later, in 1846, Macaulay toasted, 'the literature of Britain … which has exercised an influence wider than that of our commerce and mightier than that of our arms'. He went on to proclaim that 'a single shelf of a good European library was worth the whole native literature of India' (Macaulay, quoted in Whitehead 2005: 319).

Following the wave of formal independence, education became a major pillar of development assistance and, in many cases, was delivered as part of state-led formal education systems. For instance, the MDGs focused on education, with Goal 2 aimed at universal primary education. These efforts were largely successful; the Brookings Institution reported that in 2015 111 million more people completed primary school than between 1990 and 2000 (McArthur and Rasmussen 2017). However, the content of schooling remains largely Euro-focused (Silova et al. 2017). Plans such as 'Education for All' produced by UNESCO and 'Education for the Knowledge Economy' by the World Bank outline global standards based on Western ideas for primary education, human capital, and economic growth (Tikly 2009). To support these initiatives, the World Bank (branding itself the 'knowledge bank') funded textbooks and school meals and developed curricula and teacher training courses (Heyneman 2003). These initiatives have major impacts on concepts of education and teaching styles in the Global South; they influence what is taught, where it is taught, and how it is taught.

For example, Vietnam developed its National Education Strategic Development Plan 2011–20 in response to UNESCO and the World Bank's education program initiatives and the MDGs. This plan reflects the development industry's priorities of transferring Western norms and knowledge systems (Le 2020). Le (2020: 457) explains how this occurs through policies to

> (1) increase the number of teaching staffs and students trained overseas; (2) expand cooperation with foreign institutions to enhance Vietnamese institutions' capacity in both management and education, including research and professional development; and (3) attract international organizations, groups, individuals and the overseas Vietnamese to invest in and support education, participate in teaching, research and technology transfer and contribute to education reforms.

Coloniality is perpetuated by Eurocentric and Western philosophies underpinning educational systems. This coloniality of knowledge assumes universality and objectivity, and frames Western knowledge as 'the only one capable of achieving a universal consciousness', effectively dismissing non-Western knowledge as particularistic (Grosfoguel 2007: 214). Even seemingly South–South education policy transfers are often shaped by the interests of the Global North. In analysing the transfer of Colombia's Escuela Nueva education model to Vietnam, Le (2020: 461) argues that

> International organizations such as the World Bank do not only control the money; they also control alternative channels of influence through their pre-dominance in research production, international conferences organization, and the establishment of international standards and league tables. Even in cases that would appear to be South–South transfers such as Vietnam Escuela Nueva, it would be more accurate to view them as North–South–South transfers.

The measuring of education levels also warrants critical consideration since measurements can enforce standardisation and exclude those who do not fit within the criteria. Mainstream measures of educational achievement involve standardised tests and exams that label and track children. In this way, the proliferation of the quality and monitoring of education standards can become a mechanism to 'close the gap' between the 'ideal child and children who embody racialized/Othered identities' (Pérez and Saavedra 2017) such that children from marginalised position-alities are measured against white, middle-class positionalities.

Governments and development agencies that focus on 'closing the gap' rely on official statistics that reflect normative ideas about progress (Mosse 2004, 2005). This plays a crucial role in valorising particular forms of knowledge and exerting power over the poor and marginalised (Engle-Merry 2011). Therefore, we must consider how practices govern-ing education policy can result in marginalisation and exclusion, while also critically engaging with the question of what constitutes inclusion (Allan 2007: 48).

Some recent efforts have begun to develop more inclusive forms of education based on Indigenous ideas. For example, young children are now more likely to be taught in their mother tongue before moving on to another (often colonial) language of instruction (Ball 2014). Similarly, Goal 4 of the SDGs aims to 'ensure inclusive and equitable quality education and promote lifelong learning opportunities for all'. The goal's ten targets include achieving gender parity in education; providing safe learning environments and lifelong educational opportunities (primary, secondary, and tertiary education); achieving literacy and numeracy; improving teacher training; upgrading education facilities to be child, disability, and gender sensitive; and providing safe, non-violent, inclusive, and effective learning environments for all.

However, it is still necessary to ensure that community forms of education that seek to operate beyond state-based structures are recognised and supported. Paulo Freire (1970) developed one such pedagogical approach that frames education around justice, not standardisation. Freire ran classes for the Brazilian poor, especially in São Paulo, to foster the development of a critical consciousness to contest oppression, a process he called conscientisation (*conscientização* in Portuguese). In conscientisation, people dialogue about their oppression to better understand the mechanisms and structures that dehumanise and oppress them. Armed with this critical knowledge, people then visualise alternative realities of the world around them and of their own social identity to think and act from a position of empowerment. This 'pedagogy for the oppressed' (Freire 2018 [1968]) is not merely a semantic shift that leaves oppressive situations intact. Instead, conscientisation assumes that knowledge acquisition empowers people to change the environment and structures causing their subjugation. Therefore, while education rightly remains a key focus of development policies, we must continually challenge *how* education is defined, the form that it takes, and the processes by which knowledge is produced and transferred.

Challenging blueprints

The quest to improve access to employment, health care, and education appears uncontroversial. However, this chapter has underscored the need to critically reconsider these blueprints of development and forms of technical assistance. Education, health, and work discourses and policies can limit the diversity of ideas and reproduce inequalities. These dominant blueprints and technological solutions also crowd out other possibilities for human and ecological flourishing.

6   Migration and mobilities

As the COVID-19 pandemic raged across the world in 2020, lockdowns and quarantine policies restricted the movement of people as states closed their national and regional borders (Cresswell 2021). Some 'everyday mobilities were brought to an abrupt halt, while others were drastically reorganised' (Sheller 2021: 1). These restrictions, imposed by governments to contain the virus, inadvertently revealed the longstanding unevenness of movement. They exposed how 'differential mobility empowerments', reflecting 'structures and hierarchies of power' (Hannam et al. 2006: 3), have long shaped who can travel, when, where, how, and for how long (Adey et al. 2021). Importantly, the pandemic revealed entrenched inequalities surrounding different people's present and future movement, and the extent to which restrictive border measures and government policies 'endanger the lives of many vulnerable populations for whom movement is a means of survival' (Mezzadra and Stierl 2020). Unequal and disrupted movements are not new. Colonial rule, wars and conflicts, environmental destruction, poverty, and the more regularised impacts of immigration policies and visa regulations have long determined who can move, who is forced to move, and who is constrained from moving. These considerations are central to critical thinking on migration and development.

The pandemic also highlighted how bordering practices control the mobilities of (often racialised) bodies. The migration of certain groups is encouraged, while for others cross-border movements are discouraged. Creating, enforcing, transgressing, and dismantling borders of all kinds are ceaseless, pervasive processes in contemporary society and are interconnected with processes of development. Mobilities are controlled through various means, including, for example, security and surveillance along the Mexico–US wall, biometric data collection in India, the establishing and dismantling of trade barriers, the displacement of refugees, the detainment of asylum seekers, and the creation of national parks that limit human and non-human mobility. As such, bordering processes are embedded in historical, socio-spatial, and political regimes that recreate and alter borders through a wide array of material, digital, and virtual technologies.

Public debates on migration, at least in the West, tend to focus on refugees and economic migrants. However, nearly everyone is on the move or has travelled from one place to another (albeit for different lengths of time and over varying distances). Mobility thus characterises all societies. It is not exceptional or unusual, though the features and experiences of moving and staying put vary significantly over time and across societies. Migration is also not a recent phenomenon. 'The massive movement of people due to "voluntary" choice, forced removal, and economic and cultural dislocation has been one of the most prominent forces for social change over the past 500 years' (Digital History 2021). Historically, large-scale forced movements have involved enslaved people and indentured labourers, Indigenous populations expelled from their land by settler colonialism, and small-scale farmers resettled in the name of economic development. Wars and conflicts created large numbers of refugees; others moved to escape famine and extreme poverty. People also move across borders to sustain livelihoods, trade, find employment and obtain an education, or search for a better life (however conceived).

Some theorists argue that contemporary migration is unprecedented in scope, scale, geographic extent, rate of growth, and diverse character (Fortier 2014: 64). However, most migration scholars suggest that the context and form of contemporary migration is distinguishable from earlier periods by the formation of borders and border controls, processes of globalisation, rapid urbanisation, and the escalation of violent conflicts. This chapter investigates the interconnections of migration, (im)mobility, and development. It begins by presenting different definitions of migrants and migration before considering the relationship between migration and development. It then reviews more recent interventions in critical migration and mobility studies and the decolonising of migration and development.

Studying migration, mobility, and development

Mobilities is a difficult term to define. Definitions must account for forms of movement, motivations for moving, distances covered, and the diverse experiences of moving and resettling. Many analyses condense these into three main characteristics of migration: distance, time, and purpose. Thus, migration is generally defined by its motives (e.g. economic, disaster, or social), the duration and temporality of the movement (e.g. short or long term, seasonal, temporary, or permanent), the geography and distances involved (e.g. rural to urban, regional, or international), and whether the movement is voluntary or forced.

Parnwell (1993) constructed a typology of the spatial and temporal factors motivating movement. His classificatory system is often used in migration studies to map the incidences and types of migration in particular societies. However, people's motives for moving are frequently shaped by multiple conditions and considerations. Thus, typologies and definitions cannot replace more detailed analysis and rarely capture the dynamics, interconnected causes, and consequences of population movements. Furthermore, typologies of migration are often replete with problematic dichotomies (e.g. forced vs voluntary, push vs pull factors, short vs long term, and near vs far). These binaries are inadequate: for example, moving due to extreme poverty is often seen as 'voluntary', despite the social and economic circumstances compelling people to move. Therefore, even when movement is definitionally 'voluntary', the decision to move, in reality, is often determined by a context where staying *in situ* is not a realistic option. Temporal and spatial binaries are similarly fraught with limitations when determining, for example, how long someone must move to be considered a migrant, not a commuter or tourist.

The following account from an undocumented Bangladeshi migrant peddling on the streets of Barcelona reveals some of these definitional difficulties:

> I am 35 years old and come from Dhaka in Bangladesh. I have been selling scarves on the streets in Barcelona for 5 months. But I left Dhaka 8 years ago. I went first to India, then to Dubai where I worked in a restaurant, then to Austria and Germany but had to leave as I couldn't get my papers. I left and went to Italy where I sold things on the streets but couldn't get my papers there either. Now I am in Barcelona. I have applied for my papers and they say it is easier to get them here. If I do get them, I will reach my dream, which is to

go to Bradford in England where I have an uncle and get a good job there. If not, then to Belgium where I have some friends and try there. I have been to many places, but I can't stop travelling until I get my papers. It is a difficult life. (Kothari 2008: 504)

This narrative illustrates many concerns within migration studies. It confounds the idea of a single place of origin and a predetermined destination. Most movements are more complicated, involving multiple migrations and journeys, sometimes with no known destination. It also foregrounds the importance of possessing 'documents', a powerful reminder of the policies that control and constrain movement, how people navigate these limitations, and how support networks are established while on the move.

New approaches for understanding movement emerged in the 1990s within the context of increasing globalisation. These saw migration as a series of exchanges and links between different places and people (Massey 1991). As Massey (1993) argued, the emphasis should be placed on the interconnectedness of places, not only the places people move from, through, and to. As people move, they create connections between places and contribute to place-making processes. Migration was framed as a series of flows and exchanges between places (Mandel 1991) and a process through which particular social relations extend across space (King 1995). These theories also acknowledged that migration could bypass some people and places.

Appadurai (1990) offered a useful framework for understanding these networks and flows. He identified five 'scapes' of global flows that characterise migration. Ethnoscapes focus on cultural flows and the networks and connections created as people move. Financescapes are created by remittances, investments, and savings, while technoscapes involve the transfer of technology. Mediascapes involve various forms of visual, textual, and digital media that communicate particular types of knowledge, shape aspirations, and inform the opportunities available in different places. Finally, ideoscapes frame big concepts, such as democracy and human rights, and involve the transfer of lifestyles and values. Appadurai's concepts reveal how migration over time and across space can reproduce and challenge social relations of inequality and exclusion.

Understandings of migration through metaphors of flows emerged in the 1990s alongside debates on globalisation and an increasingly interconnected world (Castells 1996). Studies on transnationalism (Glick Schiller et al. 1995) also challenged static models of migration that promoted uni-directional mobility (i.e. from sending to receiving societies). They recognised more complex and multidirectional interactions between places of origin, places migrants travel through, and where they settle. After all, money, commodities, and resources move along with the migrant, with significant implications for livelihood strategies. These contributions shaped more recent understandings of the relationship between migration and development, which are explored in more detail below.

The multiple and changing terminologies labelling people who move have confounded understandings of migration. Profound political and policy implications are associated with labels such as refugees, asylum seekers, expatriates, labour migrants, settlers, or diaspora. Each term has significant social, economic, and political histories and consequences that reflect all kinds of hierarchies, privileges, and inequalities. Additionally, people's categorisations and status may shift over time (e.g. when refugees become citizens or when labour migrants lose their employment).

No universally accepted definition for 'migrant' exists at the international level. The International Organization for Migration (IOM 2019) broadly defines a migrant as

> any person who is moving or has moved across an international border or within a State away from his/her habitual place of residence, regardless of (1) the person's legal status; (2) whether the movement is voluntary or involuntary; (3) what the causes for the movement are; or (4) what the length of the stay is.

The UN suggests that the term migrant 'should be understood as covering all cases where the decision to migrate is taken freely by the individual concerned, for reasons of "personal convenience" and without intervention of an external compelling factor'. This terminology can be powerful and evocative, especially when used by the global media. Accordingly, the BBC uses the term migrant to define 'one who moves, either temporarily or permanently, from one place, area, or country of residence to another' (Ruz 2015). Meanwhile, *Al-Jazeera* elected to no longer use the term 'migrant' (where appropriate, they use 'refugee') in 2015, when many people were crossing the Mediterranean to flee conflict and poverty. The news organisation argues that the word migrant 'strips suffering people of voice' and that

> the umbrella term migrant is no longer fit for purpose when it comes to describing the horror unfolding in the Mediterranean. It has evolved from its dictionary definitions into a tool that dehumanises and distances, a blunt pejorative ... It already feels like we are putting a value on the word. Migrant deaths are not worth as much to the media as the deaths of others – which means that their lives are not. We rarely talk about the dead as individuals anymore. They are numbers ... When we in the media apply reductive terminology to people, we help to create an environment in which hate speech and thinly veiled racism can fester. (Malone 2015)

Others have also criticised the use of 'migrant' to describe people fleeing danger since the term wrongly implies a voluntary process or choice. Such definitions of migrants and understandings of migration have influenced approaches to migration and development.

Migration and development approaches

Development research and policies have long examined the interconnectedness of migration and development (de Haas 2010; Bakewell 2011). Most of this research either examines how migrants and migration generate development or how processes of development influence the form and extent of people's movement. Hammar et al. (2021) reflect on this dualistic approach, asking whether migration stimulates or obstructs development and whether development reduces or increases flows of migration.

Until recently, development agendas were based on the normative assumption that migration promotes development. For example, the migration of workers with specialised skills from the Global South was seen to boost economic productivity in the Global North. Additionally, migration was said to benefit the Global South through remittances, a redistribution of income and wealth (Kapur 2002), and improved access to educational and employment opportunities. Yet, some scholars and policy makers are pessimistic about the potential for migration to bring about positive developmental impacts. They point to the 'brain drain' effect that occurs when skilled people migrate from poorer countries and regions. This is often accompanied by a lack of opportunities to use existing skills in the places to which they move due to various forms of employment discrimination or their qualifications not being recognised. Additionally, when remittances are not forthcoming or are negligible, economic growth in migrants' places of origin is constrained and poverty and inequality persist for those left behind (de Haas 2010). At the same time, sedentarist policies that assume development can only take place when people are stilled and settled also create major challenges for communities that depend on movement for their livelihoods.

Recently, attention has turned to the 'migration–development nexus' (Nyberg-Sørensen et al. 2002), an understanding that migration and development are mutually constitutive. These studies examine the extent to which theories, approaches, and policies are founded upon varied understandings of migration as either beneficial or detrimental to development. They usually focus on remittances, brain drain, and diaspora initiatives (Raghuram 2009) or how return migration contributes to development in countries of origin via skills and knowledge transfer (Bastia and Skeldon 2020). There are multiple reasons for people to move from a position of exclusion and vulnerability to one perceived to be more inclusionary and secure. The decision to move to areas perceived to offer better opportunities can be informed by wider social changes, people's aspirations and life expectations, and higher levels of educational attainment. Thus, migration has the potential to benefit sending countries, receiving countries, migrants, and their families (though this is not without challenges).

Critical migration scholars (e.g. Faist 2007) argue that the relationship between migration and development is largely controlled by the policies of powerful states that assume migration 'can be contained, regulated or influenced' (Raghuram 2009: 104). Therefore, migration can oppress the poorest and reify inequalities (Black et al. 2006), a reality that becomes more evident when examining the multiple and varied reasons for migrating. Migration is sometimes theorised as an outcome of underdevelopment since poverty and inequality compel some to move. Delgado and Márquez Covarrubias (2009: 102) argue that studies on migration and development must 'situate the complex issues of development and underdevelopment' at the centre of their analyses. However, while migration may be motivated by escaping poverty, migrating itself can lead to further impoverishment.

To understand the role of migration in sustaining or moving out of poverty, we must consider the circumstances that make migration a successful livelihood strategy. Individuals and groups seek to improve their living conditions and transform their unequal and exclusionary position. This can be achieved by, for example, materially gaining through income-earning opportunities and the acquisition of assets or benefitting from enhanced social security systems. This can also benefit those remaining in the place of origin (i.e. through remittances). Of course, moving does not guarantee a better life. Indeed, people may move into more vulnerable situations and become further impoverished due to a lack of shelter, employment, and support systems.

Migration is often seen as a livelihood strategy for poor households, though not all amongst the poor have the option to migrate. Specific social, cultural, political, and economic characteristics shape people's decisions and choices. Certain processes and forms of inclusion and exclusion affect whether individuals and groups migrate or stay put (Kothari 2003). Harvey's (1989) notion of the 'friction of distance' is useful here. It assesses the ease or friction of movement by considering multiple interconnected factors, such as cost, migration policies, labour demand, structural and everyday discrimination, government policies, the absence of social capital within networks or contact with prospective employers, lack of knowledge about other places and opportunities beyond one's own geographical and cultural environment, social and cultural binding one to their home, physical immobility, gender, and age.

Mobility studies must also investigate those who remain because the friction of distance cannot be overcome. Those who stay in areas characterised by out-migration may also be affected by changes in access to support networks and services, remittances, and the changing household compositions that can shift the division of labour and increase the burden of care for those left behind. Mobilities need moorings (Hannam et al. 2006), as a mobile world does not replace a world of fixities. Cresswell (2010: 29) reminds us, 'to keep notions of fixity, stasis, and immobility in mind' and to consider the politics of 'obduracy' and 'friction'.

Governments and donors can have diverse, even conflictual, approaches to migration and development. Some states and policy makers see migration as desirable, while others view the movement of people unfavourably. Governments and aid donors may perceive migration as a social and economic opportunity for migrants to help develop both the societies they left and the ones they settle in, or as a constraint to development and a threat to political, economic, and social stability. States also express their identities by including or excluding others through migration policies. As such, migration 'is an arena for both deploying ideas and pursuing the day-to-day implementation and practise of policy' (Sassen 1996: 66). Paradoxically, many of the same politicians who advocate opening international borders to permit the freer movement of capital, trade, services, and technology also seek to place increasing restrictions on the movement of people. There are 'two diametrically opposed world trends. One is for greater openness of international borders ... the other is for greater restrictiveness' (Weiner 1990: 160). While these policies do control the movement of people, potential migrants are not passive recipients. Instead, borders are transgressed, and controls circumvented in multiple ways by those who want, or are compelled, to move.

The migration–development nexus framework can help us understand the interconnections between the movement of people and socio-economic change. However, understandings of mobility from the early 2000s reveal the limitations of such approaches; they are largely ahistorical and unable to fully capture the dynamic relations between migration, mobility, and development. The next section examines the possibilities of a decolonial perspective on migration, an approach that has not been fully articulated in Development Studies.

Towards migration, development, and decoloniality

The 2000s were characterised by the new mobilities paradigm developed by Sheller and Urry (2006), which shifted thinking away from flows and liquidity. They called for a new way of conceiving social relations in and through mobilities:

> mobility is historically significant and hence not unique to contemporary times: movement and spatial fixity, mobilities and immobilities, travel and borders, are always co-constituted. Therefore, the production of complex assemblages of (im)mobilities has always been a central aspect of both histor- ical and contemporary existence everywhere in the world and is always being reconfigured in complex ways to support different modes of trade, interaction, and communications ... mobility is relative with different historical concepts

being organised through specific constellations of uneven mobilities. (Sheller 2021: 10–11)

Movement is conceived as the central object of inquiry, not simply an outcome of particular social, political, and economic processes (Faulconbridge and Hui 2016: 3). In this way, 'the power and politics of discourses and practices of mobility' create both movement and stasis (Hannam et al. 2006: 3). The new mobilities approach challenges sedentarist and 'static' accounts of mobility by focusing on the 'constitutive role of movement within the workings of most social institutions and social practices' (Sheller and Urry 2016: 11).

Sheller and Urry (2006) suggest that we inhabit a world constituted by mobilities. Therefore, research on the movement of people should transcend universal and generic narratives that focus on who moves, who does not, and why. Their ideas have been widely adopted and adapted by other migration scholars. For example, Weiqiang Lin et al. (2017) examined migration infrastructures and the production of migrant mobilities to identify how organisational forces illuminate the more emergent and unfixed nature of movement.

Cresswell (2010: 18) also contributed to the new mobilities paradigm by defining mobility as involving entanglements of 'particular patterns of movement, representations of movement, and ways of practising movement'. He argued for a 'more finely developed politics of mobility that thinks below the level of mobility and immobility in terms of motive, force, speed, rhythm, route, experience, and friction' (Cresswell 2010: 21). Cresswell also introduced the idea of 'constellations of mobility' to consider the 'historically and geographically specific formations of movements, narratives about mobility and mobile practices marked by distinct forms of mobile politics and regulation'.

The new mobilities paradigm (and its iterations) has significant implications for understanding the constellations of mobility in the context of development. It also insists on adopting deeper and more extensive historical analyses. With a few notable exceptions (e.g. Chant 1998), much early migration and development research tended to homogenise migrants. However, more recent scholarship highlights social differences and explores the varied motives, experiences, and impacts of moving. These are based on, for example, gender differences (Mora and Piper

2021; Piper 2005; Willis and Yeoh 2000), intersectionality (Anthias 2012; Bastia 2014), and age and intergenerational identities (Bastia et al. 2022).

Despite this diversification, there remains a dearth of studies on migration histories and, specifically, on how understandings of the past can 'make contemporary mobilities intelligible' (Cresswell 2010: 29). This lack of historical analyses (particularly of the colonial period) tends to reproduce Eurocentric understandings of mobility (Grosfoguel et al. 2015). Becoming attuned to these histories of migration can reveal the significant and ongoing relationship between colonialism and contemporary migration (see Kothari 2009), challenge Western-centric representations of migrants, and contribute to decolonising migration studies. As Fiddian-Qasmiyeh (2020: 2) states, redressing the Eurocentrism of migration studies requires a commitment to decentring Global North knowledge of and about migration. Yet, academic research and policy reports on migration tend to focus on migration that impacts the West, reinforcing hegemonic Northern discourse about South–North migration (Crush and Chikanda 2018). It gives 'the impression that migration from the Global South to the Global North is the predominant form of migration', while more than half of all migratory movements take place between countries of the Global South (Bastia et al. 2022: 5).

Literature on historical migrations, forced movement, and imperial confinement – including slavery, indentured labour, and exiling – remains marginal in contemporary studies of migration and development. However, it can offer significant insights. For example, Sheller (2003) shows how the colonial circular movement of people and goods continues to characterise Caribbean migration today. Similarly, Benhabib (2007: 23) explores how the legacy of empire is reflected in the current rise of transnational migrations to resource-rich countries in the Global North. Other cross-disciplinary work in critical migration studies has begun to include analyses of 'race' to illuminate how immigration policies control racialised migrant bodies (Grosfoguel et al. 2015). More recently, important research focusing on Indigenous (im)mobilities addresses the contradictions and tensions around of the notion of 'settling' in the context of settler colonialism and Indigenous mobility (Carpio et al. 2022). These spatial contradictions, of settling and mobility, are evident as Indigenous populations are driven off the land and subsequently confined to reservations so that Europeans can move in and settle. Carpio et al. (2022: 179) introduce the concepts of 'settler anchoring' and 'mobility sovereignty' to contend that 'settler colonial spaces are structures of mobility injustice, and that securing Indigenous mobility must account for the ability of Indigenous peoples to choose when, where, how, and for what purposes to engage in movement'. Indeed, as Sheller (2018: 28) writes, 'mobility is deeply connected to ideas of freedom, individualism, and liberalism; ideas that have historically shaped and structured uneven spatial relations within a mobile ontology'. Similarly, Katz (2022: 220) investigates mobility injustice in the context of settler colonialism, writing that 'settler colonialism was and still is based on two complementary movements of expansion and expulsion, that is, the movement of settlers to "new" territories and the imposed movement, or rather displacement, of local populations within or from these territories'.

These understandings of settling and mobility remind us how the capacity to decide who can move, who can settle, where, and under what conditions is always political (Mbembe 2019) and that 'wherever there is mobility there always will be turbulence' (Cresswell 2014: 719). Critical migration studies and decolonial scholarship are beginning to reframe understandings of migration and mobilities (see Favell 2022). They recognise how historical, specifically colonial, (im)mobility injustices pervade the present and reject the reproduction of these (Vanyoro 2019). In the context of development, Raghuram (2009: 113) argues that disrupting the 'cosy relationship' between migration and development requires us to 'recognise how migration is central to constituting the paradigm of development'. Migration is an increasingly important topic among Development Studies scholars, policy makers, and researchers. Yet, much scholarship on the links between migration and development has not fully engaged with more critical debates and insights emerging out of the new mobilities research paradigm and the decolonial approaches reviewed above.

7 Degradation and sustainability

The 26th meeting of the 'Conference of the Parties' (COP26) was held in Glasgow, Scotland, in 2021. At the first COP, the 1992 Earth Summit in Rio de Janeiro, 197 governments signed the United Nations (UN) Framework Convention on Climate Change. Participants aimed to rethink economic development and find ways to halt the destruction of irreplaceable natural resources and the pollution of the planet. The original Framework Convention has been revised and refined over the years to secure global agreements and action to address the negative effects of human activities on climate systems.

Over the past 20 years, climate science has produced compelling evidence that human actions are significantly changing the composition of the atmosphere and altering the functioning of the climate system (Intergovernmental Panel on Climate Change [IPCC] 2007). The IPCC is the preeminent global research body producing science on the changing climate. To stop climate change from rising above 1.5 °C, the IPCC determined (in 2018) that global net anthropogenic CO_2 emissions needed to decline by 45 per cent from 2010 levels by 2030 and reach net zero around 2050. To keep the planet below 1.5 °C, global emissions of carbon dioxide needed to have peaked by 2020. The IPCC set the critical limit of 1.5 °C above pre-industrial temperatures to keep the planet habitable and avoid catastrophic climate change. Temperatures above this risk hitting 'tipping points', irreversible damage that locks the planet into disastrous changes.

However, by 2018, the planet was already at 1 °C above pre-industrial levels. The IPCC's 2018 report explained that global warming was likely to reach 1.5 °C between 2030 and 2052 at current rates. This 12-year window was the moment to take well-overdue action (Frankel 2018). However, in 2021, just before COP26 in Glasgow, the IPCC reported that little progress had been made in curbing climate change. They issued a 'code red for humanity', meaning that (barring immediate and drastic action) limiting global warming to 1.5 °C or even 2 °C above pre-industrial levels 'will be beyond reach' within the next two decades.

Biodiversity loss, environmental degradation, and climate change are at the core of current sustainable development concerns. For example, the 2030 Agenda for Sustainable Development, articulated as part of the Sustainable Development Goals, 'is a plan of action for people, planet and prosperity'. It reflects the interlinkages between three foundational imperatives of development – social, economic, and environmental sustainability. However, these goals are often in conflict, and attempts to simultaneously achieve all three are fraught with tensions. For example, the pursuit of economic growth through industrialisation and large-scale development projects (e.g. building dams and coal mining) has degraded the physical environment. Similarly, policies implemented to protect the environment may have negative social and economic consequences if they result in Indigenous people being pushed off their land. Therefore, climate change, biodiversity loss, and environmental degradation present immense global challenges that require profound shifts in development discourses and practices. This chapter examines these concerns and tensions. It first explores how development processes have led to environmental degradation before reviewing critical approaches that can promote environmental sustainability.

Development and degradation

Two longstanding core tenets inform development's understanding of and engagement with the 'natural' world. The first is separating the human from the non-human world and seeking supremacy over it. The second is the tendency to imagine economic growth as compatible with environmental sustainability. Both contribute to environmental degradation.

Environmental degradation and human/non-human distinctions

An ongoing challenge for development is its belief in human superiority over nature and distinctions between humans and non-humans. This disconnection has enabled exploitation, expropriation, and supremacy over the natural environment and non-humans. Typically, the value assigned to whole ecologies and animals is based on their profitability (e.g. how much money can be made by turning an 'empty' plot into a housing development, or a cow's skin into a handbag?). Yet, this quest to accumulate profits from the natural environment and non-human beings is also driving our potential extinction from climate change and mass biodiversity loss (Hage 2017).

The conceptual disconnection between humans and 'nature' has its roots in Enlightenment thinking. This period was characterised by liberal individualistic thought, the industrial revolution, and declarations of individual rights (Douzinas 2000). Racial and anthropogenic hierarchies and separation from nature were considered modern (Douzinas 2000). This thinking fuelled the colonial projects of European empires, where exploitation of the racialised 'other' cemented the idea that civilisation was apart from nature. Enlightenment thinkers were oblivious to other sophisticated worldviews that saw the natural world as having value or meaning beyond its instrumentalised use. This is particularly true of Indigenous worldviews, which have intricate, entwined, and detailed relations with nature (Mignolo 2011).

This disconnect between humans and ecologies deepened with the industrial revolution and the unrestrained productivity, resource extraction, and commodification of capitalism. Since the industrial revolution, there has been unparalleled mass exploitation of ecologies and non-humans, as well as other human beings. Indeed, economic growth often relies on extraction, destruction, and degradation of the natural world. As Castree (1995: 12) writes,

> Capitalism commodifies whole landscapes, constructs and reconstructs them in particular (profit motivated) ways ... The imperatives of capitalism bring all manner of natural environments and concrete labor processes upon them together in an abstract framework of market exchange. Under capitalism humans relate to nature in a specific way, through commodification of natural products, and in so doing actively appropriate, transform, and creatively destroy it.

'Nature' then is seen as separate from 'society' and is envisaged as something to be controlled and commodified.

The concept of the Anthropocene captures the rapidly accumulating impacts of these kinds of human activity on non-humans and environmental processes. The Anthropocene, which situates humanity in a geological temporal frame, is typically conceived as the period since Western industrialisation and colonisation, at most 250 years in the making (Tyszczuk 2016). Humans are imagined as a geological force that will leave traces of their presence and destruction in future stratigraphic formations (Rickards 2015). While the idea of the Anthropocene has been useful in marking human impacts on the environment, it can also be misleading. Indigenous societies existed well before this period and did not bring about such ecological devastation. Indigenous peoples across the world have long noted the problematic and destructive relationship between colonial powers (later, liberal states) and the natural world. Thus – and this is critical for development – not all humans are equally culpable since some ways of living are more destructive than others. As the environmental historian Jason Moore (2017) suggests, the term 'Capitalocene' may be more appropriate since climate change and enduring patterns of inequality are linked to the global capitalist economy.

Development and sustainability

Development concerns about the relationship between humans and the environment build on a longstanding history of environment-related issues. Importantly, Indigenous knowledge has always been rooted in deep connections with land, natural resources, and ecosystems. Indigenous people's interactions with the natural world are

> embedded in a cosmology that reveres the *one-ness* of life, considers nature as sacred and acknowledges humanity as a part of it. And it encompasses practical ways to ensure the balance of the environment in which they live, so it may continue to provide services such as water, fertile soil, food, shelter and medicines. (Drissi 2020, emphasis in original)

However, these understandings of the relationship between humans and non-humans have, until recently, been largely invisible to development planners and policy makers. Now, such ways of knowing and living with the environment are beginning to be more widely acknowledged. For example, the United Nations Permanent Forum on Indigenous Issues, established in 2000, argues that Indigenous people's contributions are essential in designing and implementing ecosystem solutions.

Despite centuries-old Indigenous knowledge, early environmental and development concerns were informed by Thomas Malthus's famous work, *An Essay on the Principle of Population* (1798). Malthusians and neo-Malthusians specifically focused on overpopulation and resource depletion. In 1972, *The Limits of Growth* was published by a group of economists who considered how five variables had changed over time: population growth, food output, natural resources, industrial output, and pollution (Meadows et al. 1972). Their scenarios predicted that humanity would see a collapse in the earth's carrying capacity by the middle of the 21st century. While these are important topics to consider, the focus on population growth in the Global South, not on consumption patterns in the Global North, shifted the blame away from those most responsible for climate change. More worryingly, it legitimised racist and eugenic ideas of population control.

Three key conferences on environment and development (Stockholm, 1972; Rio de Janeiro, 1992; and Johannesburg, 2002) brought governments together to map out a program for 'sustainable development'. The first significant definition of sustainable development was put forward in the Brundtland Report titled *Our Common Future* (Brundtland 1987). This report, mandated by the UN, aimed to formulate realistic proposals to address environmental and development concerns. It defined sustainable development as 'development that meets the needs of the present without compromising the ability of future generations to meet their own needs' (292). This represents the first major linking of development, climate change, and environmental destruction on the international stage. However, the report was criticised for not detailing the causes of environmental degradation, including how it was largely due to the consumption and production practices of rich and industrialised countries and peoples. Furthermore, it failed to outline who was responsible for addressing environmental harm, and it did not offer concrete remedies. The depoliticisation of responsibility for environmental harm has been an enduring criticism of sustainable development, especially since industrialised nations continue to degrade the environment through a relentless quest for economic growth. Critics often frame sustainable development as little more than a set of reformist ideas seeking to reconcile development, economic growth, and the deterioration and destruction of the natural world.

Sustainable development typically presents technological innovations, including better ecological management, as important for alleviating the pressures of economic growth. These claims assert that science can resolve resource, environmental, and ecological crises by rapidly developing advanced technologies. Yet, environmentalists argue that contemporary capitalist practices have led to rapid and dramatic environmental and climate change. As Boris Frankel (2018: 2) writes in *Fictions of Sustainability*, 'No matter how many innovative products and technologies, new forms of management and marketing, or the expansion of markets beyond the local and the national to the global, capitalism as the incessant accumulation of capital … is unsustainable'. The (African) Green Revolution offers an instructive example to explore why technological transfer is a tenuous promise (Clay and King 2019). The original Green Revolution was driven by the Rockefeller Foundation through a project in Mexico in the 1950s. It then expanded across Asia with the support of multilateral development organisations. The aim was to increase production of food grains, especially wheat and rice, in an attempt to alleviate poverty and hunger. The 1970s and 1980s saw rapid growth in agricultural outputs associated with the introduction of Western technological inputs, such as high-yielding seed varieties, fertilisers, pesticides, and various agro-engineering technologies, such as terracing, draining wetlands, and irrigating.

Yet, despite some early successes, the impacts of the first Green Revolution were ultimately ruinous for local populations and ecologies. The intense focus on technology transfer to increase yield overlooked other social, economic, and ecological impacts. The new varieties required large amounts of chemical fertilisers and pesticides that were environmentally harmful and costly. The first Green Revolution concentrated capital away from poor farmers and their governments (who paid for the technologies and additional agricultural inputs) into the hands of multinational agricultural companies. These companies made the seeds that required *their* fertilisers, so farmers in the Global South became reliant on products purchased from these multilaterals (Patel 2013). These new technologies also damaged ecosystems by crowding out and reducing Indigenous crop varieties and poisoning the land with harmful pesticides and fertilisers (Cleaver 1972). Additionally, some older strains were better adapted to local conditions.

The contemporary hyperfocus on technological solutions to climate change, without dealing with unrestrained economic growth, is reminiscent of such mistakes. It is becoming increasingly evident that technology alone cannot solve future ecological, economic, and social crises. Thus, sustainable development could not resolve the tension between economic growth and environmental destruction. Rather, discourses of sustainable development have tried to

> save global capitalist society from the unintended consequences of its own success at expanding production. But ecological problems and environmental degradation have continued to worsen during the more than twenty years since the promulgation of the sustainable development formula ... the forest industry continues to destroy the remaining strands of natural forest; industrial agricultural practices are destroying the fertility of the soil; overfishing and ocean pollution are wiping out the world's fish stocks; massive new hydro projects continue in sensitive areas; there is renewed government support for nuclear industry. (O'Malley and Clow 2011: 216)

Sustainable development approaches seeking to address climate change have had mixed results. Critics challenge its apolitical framing of climate change, arguing that climate change is not a purely physical phenomenon but should also be seen as a cultural concept (Hulme 2008). Other critical scholars adopt a political economy (Tanner and Allouche 2011) approach to climate change; some also focus on the realm of the 'everyday' and societal perceptions of climate change (Artur and Hilhorst 2012; Kothari and Arnall 2019).

Despite these alternative approaches, the extraction of fossil fuels continues to provide rich financial rewards for oil, gas, and coal companies that consider environmental impacts to be subsidiary political concerns. Gibson and Warren (2020) outline the difficulty of aligning environmental rhythms with the unpromising capitalist rhythms of investment and profit return. The 'limits of growth' remain a major concern for contemporary development and tensions between economic growth and environmental destruction persist. Indeed, the perpetuation of capitalism (i.e. expropriation, exploitation, consumption, accumulation, and growth) severely constrains attempts to address environmental crises. Yet, new theories and approaches for addressing environmental degradation and sustainability have emerged to critique mainstream thinking on climate change and environmental management. These include political ecology approaches, degrowth, climate justice, and *Buen Vivir*, each of which is discussed below.

Political ecology

Political ecology emerged in the 1970s to critique hitherto apolitical accounts of ecology and expose the serious conceptual and empirical limitations of sustainable development (see Bryant 1998; Peet and Watts 1996; Robbins 2019). It examines environment–society relations and political struggles over access to natural resources, and foregrounds how dominant accounts of environmental crisis and ecological change ignore political-economic forces. Political ecology is not necessarily *more* political, but it is more explicit about the politics underpinning the assumptions and goals of environmental sustainability. Political ecologists argue that any attempt to place a monetary value on environmental systems will entrench inequalities (Sikor 2013). They advocate centring the redistribution of power and resources, not financial valuations and certainly not controlling population growth. They also challenge the assertion that modern technologies and markets can optimise production while simultaneously ensuring environmental benefits (see the Green Revolution, Lal et al. 2002). Environmental knowledge transferred wholesale from the Global North to the Global South is often inappropriate and ignores or marginalises more relevant Indigenous and local environmental knowledge and practices (Uphoff 1988).

Robbins (2019) identifies several common themes of political ecology scholarship. First, political ecology positions degradation and sustainability within the wider global political economy and, importantly, in the context of modernisation approaches to development (Blaikie and Brookfield 1987). This challenges the notion that marginal people are to be blamed for environmental degradation. Rather, development efforts to improve production levels often result in locally unsustainable practices (Kane 2012). Second, political ecology problematises supposedly benign national parks and biodiversity zones that do not acknowledge local and historical struggles over territory, resources, and landscapes (Beymer-Farris and Bassett 2012). Third, political ecology reveals how environmental conflict is founded upon unequal access to resources, and how this is shaped by class, gender, and ethnic inequalities. An increasing scarcity of resources (e.g. if state authorities enclose or appropriate resources) can exacerbate conflicts between various local groups (Moore 2008). These concerns have created spaces for new forms of environmental activism and new political identities linked to social struggles. As Maldonado-Villalpando et al. (2022: 1301) remind us, the 'environmental failure of successive Western development models imposed on the Global South has led local communities to pursue alternatives to development'. These include movements such as the Zapatistas in Mexico or the Chipko movement in India (see Bebbington and Batterbury 2001; Hernández et al. 2020).

Political ecology approaches challenge Western environmental knowledge and link local ecologies to wider global political and economic processes. However, Sultana (2021) maintains that political ecology has largely been produced within, and remains bound to, colonial or settler colonial spaces of knowledge production. Although political ecology often defines itself against Eurocentric conceptions, it has also contributed to the reproduction of globally uneven geographies of knowledge (Wainwright 2008). Ironically, environmental restoration and protection efforts that fail to understand local histories of inequality can lead to further degradation, marginalisation, and control over community resources. To address this continuing Eurocentrism, Loftus (2019: 178) advocates decolonising political ecology by theorising 'from situated, relationally understood sets of socio-ecological practices'.

Political ecology has begun integrating the voices of previously marginalised people from diverse communities (Bryant 2015). Specifically, feminist political ecology (see Harcourt and Nelson 2015) has helped to 'better understand the everyday, embodied, and emotional aspects of nature-society relations' and 'attend to gender and uneven power relations in environmental struggles, gendered environmental knowledges, rights, and practices, as well as gendered environmental movements and collectivities' (Sultana 2021: 156). Going forward, political ecology must engage more deeply with Indigenous (see Zanotti et al. 2020), decolonial, and feminist scholarship to further shape development research practices and environmental policies.

Degrowth and dealing with capitalism

Economic growth plays a central role in capitalist understandings of economic success. It is considered necessary to reduce unemployment, decrease debt, and fund public services (Kallis et al. 2018). Consequently, it is widely assumed that economic development fosters increases in well-being. However, since the 1970s, and especially in the 2000s, scholars have questioned this rationale by illustrating how processes of growth can create economic, social, and environmental crises (Kallis et al. 2012). To address this persistent problem, recent scholarship has introduced the idea of 'degrowth'.

Degrowth describes a transition beyond capitalism, a different political-economic system in which societies use radically fewer natural resources and 'organize and live differently than today' (Kallis 2015: 3). These alternatives are essentially non-capitalist since they diminish the importance of core capitalist institutions. Instead, they focus on the reproductive economy of care, the reclaiming of old – and the creation of new – commons, eco-communities, and cooperatives, and the redistribution of wealth and resources. In doing so, degrowth counters the long-perpetuated equivalence of growth and progress (Kallis 2011). However, degrowth is not universally transferable; high-income countries that exceed per capita fair-shares of planetary boundaries must do the most degrowth to reduce excess resource and energy use (Hickel 2019b). Meanwhile, poorer countries can continue increasing resource and energy use within planetary boundaries to meet human needs (Hickel 2020).

The impacts of climate change are unequally produced and felt. Extreme weather events, heat stress, rising sea levels, forced displacement, and infections and diseases are just a few of the dangers already affecting poor, vulnerable populations in developing countries. Despite this, climate change policies often overlook the priorities of the poorest and even place additional stress on already vulnerable communities. Those with the least social and economic capital available to mitigate environmental degradation are often the most vulnerable. People with the fewest resources are left in disinvested environments as more mobile and wealthier people move out. Importantly, those most affected by climate change, often the poorest and those residing in the Global South, have contributed least to climate change. Wealthy countries and individuals with high-consumption and CO_2-producing lifestyles are major polluters yet they have the resources to protect themselves. Therefore, the question of responsibility lies at the heart of deliberations on climate change (Hickel 2020).

Dengler and Seebacher (2019: 248) outline how degrowth risks recreating coloniality by reproducing

> longstanding (neo-)colonial asymmetries by (once again!) setting the agenda on what ought to be done to solve problems of global relevance in the Global North. This happens without negotiating the aspired transformation on equal footing with the Global South, which is thereby (once again!) rendered dependent on Western benevolence.

Dengler and Seebacher (2019: 251) argue that a decolonial degrowth approach should 'elaborate on an inherently feminist and decolonial metatheoretical foundation ... exhibit integrative and relational ontologies of societal embeddedness in nature and de-ontologize false dichotomies'. Hickel (2020) outlines how degrowth can guide economies towards sovereignty, self-sufficiency, and human well-being, while creating conceptual and practical space for societies to find their own trajectories and definitions of the good life (Kallis 2015). This requires acknowledging political projects in the Global South that represent alternatives to development and alternative socio-economic systems, such as *'Buen Vivir'* in Latin America (i.e. Sumak Kawsay in Ecuador), Ubuntu in South Africa, or the Gandhian Economy of Permanence in India. These philosophies have reinvigorated calls to better integrate knowledge and perspectives on degrowth 'from the margins' (Hanaček et al. 2020).

Buen Vivir and Earth rights

While the West was leading the world to ecological demise, others were forging important alternative pathways. Indigenous movements in Ecuador have long mobilised around the Kichwa concept of *sumak kawsay* or *Buen Vivir*, loosely meaning the 'good life'. This worldview fundamentally recentres the interconnectedness and wholeness of life and, in so doing, rejects the divide between humans and non-humans. Global Studies scholar Miriam Lang (2019: 177) describes the tenets of *Buen Vivir*:

> Instead of unlimited material accumulation, *Buen Vivir* proposes equilibrium, balance and harmony as the highest values of coexistence. Instead of being pursued as a goal, accumulation of material wealth or individual power is considered a threat to the community, and its possibilities are systematically deactivated by mechanisms of redistribution, reciprocity and rotation of duties.

At the same time, communitarian life is not fixed in tradition, but evolves according to the needs of all, in situated historical processes actively shaped by collective deliberation. Instead of competition, *Buen Vivir* proposes collaboration. Instead of the capitalist *homo oeconomicus*, always rationally interested in getting the best for just himself, it proposes an ontology of being collectively, in community, in awareness of our deep interdependences with other human and non-human beings. Instead of dividing life into different realms of the social, the political and the economical, it conceives life as a whole. Instead of defining nature as a set of resources external to human life and prone to exploitation, it defines human life as a part of all forms of life as a whole.

Buen Vivir is much more than simply 'culture' or ideology. Latin American scholars and activists Mónica Chuji, Grimaldo Rengifo, and Eduardo Gudynas (2019: 111) suggest it 'expresses a deeper change in knowledge, affectivity, and spirituality, an ontological opening to other forms of understanding the relationship between humans and non-humans which do not imply the modern separation between society and nature'.

In 2007, Rafael Correa's progressive government was elected in Ecuador and wrote *Buen Vivir* into the constitution the next year. This significant moment legally bequeathed rights to non-human entities, such as rivers and forests. Specifically, Article 71 stated that nature, 'has the right to integral respect for its existence and for the maintenance and regeneration of its life cycles, structure, functions and evolutionary processes' (Tănăsescu 2017: 433). The right to restoration and regeneration was also granted, meaning that Ecuadorian authorities had to enforce the rights of nature, not solely those of humans.

While the granting of rights to nature has been celebrated, *Buen Vivir* has suffered setbacks since its operationalisation into the constitution. It has been subjected to the efficiency and management logics of the neoliberal state, which often overlooks the rights of nature when approving profitable extractive and mining projects. Nonetheless, as Lang (2019) has documented, some local governments and authorities have successfully used *Buen Vivir* to reorder life in their communities. *Buen Vivir* is asserted beyond the confines of the state and, therefore, continues to offer hope to communities in Ecuador and beyond.

Buen Vivir is sometimes reduced to a post-neoliberal official state project in Ecuador and Bolivia (and, briefly, Venezuela). Yet, *Buen Vivir* and its Indigenous-language variations (*sumak kawsay* in Quechua and *sumaq qamaña* in Aymara) go beyond post-neoliberal government policies; they represent a novel post-development, decolonial discourse, and practice.

As these approaches illustrate, the sustainable environment is at the core of humanity's future. Indeed, the recent COVID-19 pandemic provides a powerful example of 'how human health and ecosystem health are closely intertwined – and how human systems are dependent on natural systems' (Uitto 2021: 3). Yet, as Edensor et al. (2019: 258) write,

> despite a widely articulated discourse of despair and societal decline in accordance with environmental concerns, there is also hope. This is manifest in the possibilities that future generations might act in progressive ways in contradistinction to the idea that they will only be passive victims of such changes. As such, our imagining of the future cannot be overdetermined by our assumptions about the past.

Ultimately, approaches to sustainable development must account for political economy and power (Adams 2019). Additionally, as Head (2016: 57) argues in *Hope and Grief in the Anthropocene,*

> for those of us who grew up with Western thinking, our most profound and important challenge is the challenge of reconceptualising human relations to the more-than-human world. It will not occur as a purely cerebral activity, but as a process of engagement with the dilemmas of everyday practice.

She argues for grieving the loss of the modern self and environment. However, grief alone is insufficient if it becomes disempowering. Rather, it must engender a 'gritty, keeping-going kind of hope' to be practised, not simply felt (Head 2016: 11).

8 Towards solidarity, decoloniality, and building the pluriverse

Introduction

This book was composed at a particularly challenging global moment, shaped by climate injustice, the COVID-19 pandemic, the war in Ukraine and other ongoing violent conflicts, growing inequalities, and environmental destruction. Such events and challenges remind us that development problems are becoming increasingly global, interconnected, complex, and multifaceted. Accordingly, they demand new approaches. The critical thinking presented in the previous chapters unsettles dominant discourses of development, confronts colonial inheritances, and reorients understandings of injustices. It draws on critical theories to challenge hierarchical classifications and categorisations of people and places, address the ahistoricity of development, and confound spatial distinctions.

There has always been resistance to dispossession and the concentration and exercise of power. In this sense, alternative possibilities are already underway (see Demaria and Kothari 2017). However, when no environmental disaster, health crisis, or conflict is alarming enough to fundamentally change the structures and systems that create and maintain inequalities, then new development tools and possibilities are needed to counter deep injustices. There is no single, simple solution to the challenges of our time, only ways to unsettle development. In this concluding chapter, we offer five possibilities for further research, practice, and action: solidarity and justice, decoloniality, redistribution, reparations, and the pluriverse.

Towards solidarity and justice

Most development discourse and practice continue to create disparities, undermine notions of unity, and frustrate attempts to achieve social justice. However, recent global anti-colonial campaigns and protests brought us to a critical moment replete with potential to shape the future and build new forms of solidarity.

Featherstone (2012: 12) sees solidarity as a 'transformative relation' between places and different social groups. While there exist 'many different uses of solidarity by elite ... as well as subaltern and working-class movements', solidarity here refers to the transformative relations forged through political struggles that seek 'to challenge forms of oppression' (Featherstone 2012: 5). Solidarity is committed to forging practices of care and confronting structural injustice, activities that also constitute the foundational tenets of critical development practice. Yet, in seeking to instil solidaristic principles and promote new forms of solidarity, we must remain vigilant and confront historical relations that continue to shape lives and worlds today. This reconsideration of development requires recognising the multiple, intimate, and public spaces from which solidarity can emerge and the various ways it can be expressed (e.g. by individuals and collectives; amid the rhythms of everyday life and at in critical moments). Acts of solidarity are always political, regardless of which form they take and in which spaces they manifest. In this section, we consider the relationship between development and notions of solidarity before exploring how new forms of solidarity might be created in the context of development.

There remains a taken-for-granted assumption that the development industry exemplifies solidarity inherent in its North–South connections and proclaimed commitments to universal justice, rights, and care for distant others (Yanacopulos and Smith 2007). However, despite the SDGs' renewed commitment to partnerships, development thinking and practice generally remains anti-solidaristic. Furthermore, building connections is not necessarily foundational to development: instead it has been shown to create and reproduce racial, moral, geographical, technical, political, and cultural distinctions and hierarchies.

Popular ideas about solidarity have been reconfigured by the proliferation of development-related campaigns in the West that promote charitable causes and expand public (and celebrity) involvement (Brockington 2014). This public discourse of solidarity, in and of the West, illustrates what Chouliaraki (2013: 180) calls 'cool capitalism [that] replaces conviction with consumption'. These shifts, masquerading as solidarity, emerge from neoliberal ideologies privileging consumption, individualism, and utilitarianism. Doing good to others is geared towards personal fulfilment (Chouliaraki 2013). Narratives of solidarity that may have previously been expressed by collective movements are now being replaced by individualist projects. Moreover, consuming solidaristically can shift the gaze away from violence and oppression by encouraging Western publics to 'shop well to save the world' (Richey and Ponte 2011). This seriously limits possibilities for ethically and politically driven interventions to transform relations of injustice and inequality. As Chouliaraki (2011:364) suggests, solidarity can no longer be understood as 'the imperative to act towards vulnerable others without the anticipation of reciprocation'. Other scholars concur, arguing that those purportedly acting to support the oppressed are largely motivated by instrumental self-interest (Barnett and Weiss 2008). Their interventions potentially reinforce unequal relations between the supporter and the sufferer (Fortier 2014).

As the burgeoning solidarity economy emerges, development is also becoming increasingly commercialised, professionalised, and bureaucratised (Kothari 2005). Chouliaraki suggests these changes reflect three transformations: the instrumentalisation of development and aid, the retreat of grand narratives of solidarity, and the reshaping of social realities by communication technologies. Thus, solidarity is no longer a political engagement with human vulnerability. The former secretary-general of the United Nations, Ban Ki-moon, highlighted this concern when he argued that the 2015 Mediterranean refugee crisis was an absence of solidarity, not a crisis of numbers; it demonstrated the social inability to forge practices of care for others based on recognition and responsibility. Additionally, much Western media increased its 'affective labour' to effectively replace solidarity with a politics of fear (supporting Chouliaraki's transformations in communications).

Other critics identify an absence of real solidarity around issues of justice. As Fassin (2017) argues, we must move beyond critiquing individual actions and motives as misguided or selfish. Instead, we must focus on the unequal historical and structural conditions and access to resources that create and perpetuate inequalities. Indeed, distinguishing between those 'vulnerable others seen as worthy of our emotions and those that are perceived as unworthy' (Chouliaraki 2013: 23) is partly shaped by historical, specifically racialised and colonial, depictions persistently reproduced through embedded ideas of cultural superiority (Kothari 2006b). These reified distinctions between people and places (see Chapter 4) make it increasingly difficult to forge a shared humanity. In this context, Massey (2002) calls for a politics of interrelation that focuses on how difference is constructed through historical and contemporary relationships of exclusion, oppression, and privilege. Such analyses would be 'concerned with challenging, and taking responsibility for, the form of the relationships through which identities are constructed, in which we are individually and collectively positioned and through which society more broadly is constituted' (Massey 2002: 284).

Despite much work on solidarity and development, there is an ongoing need to consider what would constitute a radical reconceptualisation of solidaristic development and explore how development can create spaces for these new forms of solidarity to be viable and sustainable.

We argue that development ideas underpinned by solidaristic principles can support political struggles to transform relations of inequality, violence, and dispossession. This necessitates investigating real-world contexts in which solidarity has emerged, whether serendipitously, by design, or a combination of both. We need to explore which connections and understandings between people contribute to the emergence of solidaristic emotions, practices, and behaviours and what obstacles confound such outcomes. Solidarity should not only be invoked at distinct critical moments, in the grand mission statements of global charities, or within the criteria for the disbursal of development aid through the SDGs. Rather, solidarity can emerge over time by speaking truth and relinquishing power and in convivial encounters of everyday life.

Critically, during times of social and political upheaval, cultural shifts, and economic instability, solidarity must entail a willingness to redistribute material and immaterial resources (see Stjernø 2004; Federici 2012). One example of such solidarity that has recently gained renewed momentum is the repatriation of stolen and appropriated colonial objects. As McAuliffe writes (2021: 678), 'the present moment sees a wide-ranging and unprecedented reckoning in European societies with their colonial pasts and with the related question of how the racist legacies of imperialism resound today'. For example, in 2019, Manchester Museum partnered with the Australian Institute of Aboriginal and Torres Strait Islander Studies (AIATSIS) to begin returning sacred artefacts to Indigenous aboriginal communities through the 'Return of Cultural Heritage' project. Such items were taken by force during colonisation and would never have been given over willingly. The Curator of Manchester Museum, Stephen Welsh, acknowledged that 'Western processes and protocols established to catalogue, preserve and analyse objects and specimens in isolation from traditional owners, countries of origin and diaspora communities, continues to inflict loss, trauma and exclusion on those people most closely connected with collections' (Ward 2019).

This was recognised by the CEO of the AIATSIS, who stated that the repatriation of objects 'fosters truth telling about our Nation's history'. A representative of the Native Title Aboriginal Corporation added that the 'repatriation of our sacred cultural heritage items is a fundamental part of the healing process' as 'locked deep within these items is our lore; our histories, our traditions and our stories'. Powerful themes of global solidarity emerged at the repatriation ceremony. The museum's director, Esme Ward, emphasised that a museum should foster 'thinking about our common humanity'. This was affirmed by Mangubadijarri Yanner, one of the Traditional Owners, who explained 'we share a dark history – but it's moments like this, when we come together as one, united by our desire to do better, to be better and to right the wrongs of the past, that we start to heal spiritual hurts and the intergenerational trauma that still exists today' (Ward, 2019).

In July 2022, Germany and Nigeria signed an agreement to return hundreds of artefacts that were looted and removed by the British during colonialism and later auctioned off to Germany. On the day of the signing, a representative of the German Green party stated, 'today we have reason to celebrate because we have reached an agreement on the Benin bronzes … It was wrong to take the bronzes and it was wrong to keep them. This is the beginning to right the wrongs' (Oltermann 2022). Parzinger, the head of the Prussian Cultural Heritage Foundation, further acknowledged that the agreement represented a significant milestone in reappraising colonial injustices. The Smithsonian Institution subsequently announced that it would also return most of the Benin bronzes in its possession.

The return of stolen objects offers one example of the potential to develop progressive, transformational, decolonial forms of solidarity. Solidarity can emerge in multiple spaces and be expressed in various ways: for example, giving 'support to those who are willing to expose the will of the institution as violence' (Ahmed 2017: 159), coming together in public assembly to protest (Butler 2015), interrogating hegemonic discourses, repatriating stolen objects, or challenging practices that oppress. Noxolo (2017: 342) suggests that decolonial theory can support this project by providing a loud and radical challenge that directly protests and confronts existing practices. We now turn to potential decolonial futures for development.

Towards decolonising development

Mignolo (2020) reminds us that calls for decoloniality are not new – they have existed for at least 500 years (from South American resistance against European invasion). However, recent global campaigns and movements have reinvigorated demands to decolonise. This presents a critical moment, replete with potential, for development discourse, policy, and action.

Decolonising is currently high on official academic agendas, with much talk about how to decolonise the university, curriculum, and other colonising structures. Yet, as Wilson (2001: 214) reminds us, true decolonisation must be concerned with 'a more critical understanding of the underlying assumptions, motivations and values that inform research practices'. Said also emphasised the importance of critically interrogating and reflecting on internalised value systems, writing: 'underlying every interpretation of other cultures is the choice facing the individual scholar or intellectual; whether to put intellect at the service of power or at the service of criticism, communities, and moral sense' (Said 1981: 164). Similarly, Claire Galien (2020: 40) stresses:

> The decolonial approach does not restrict itself to a critique of the colonial episteme and world order. It entails a recognition of one's own positionality as scholar, critic, and speaker, recognizes the necessity to decenter and pluralise knowledge formations, and finally offers alternative ways to conceptualize and experience the world. Thus, decoloniality is best described as a gesture that de-normalizes the normative, problematizes default positions, debunks

the a-perspectival, destabilizes the structure, and as a program to rehabilitate epistemic formations that continue to be repressed under coloniality.

However, Tuck and Yang (2012: 1) reiterate that decolonisation 'is not a metaphor for other things we want to do to improve our societies and schools' but must 'bring about the repatriation of Indigenous land and life'. Decolonising then goes beyond interrogating individual positionality and forms of knowledge production – it must be material. This entails returning appropriated resources and undoing economic structures that reproduce colonial inequalities. Scholars have long understood how capitalist economic systems dehumanise populations and legitimise devaluation, expropriation, and dispossession through racism (Amin 1976; Fraser 2016; Mills 2007; Hall 1980; Rodney 1972). Yet, many remain reluctant to perform the critical, material work of redistribution and reparation so powerfully articulated by Tuck and Yang (2012). Without such work, 'decolonial theory can become yet another instrument for time-honoured colonialist manoeuvres of discursively absenting, brutally exploiting and then completely forgetting Indigenous people' (Noxolo 2017: 343).

The project of decolonising development has recently gained significant momentum. For example, scholars have called for decolonising global health (Fofana 2021), justice, human rights, and peacebuilding (Benyera 2022; Schirch 2022), and Development Studies education (Patel and North 2022). However, there is some disquiet as to how decolonising development is being promoted and understood and by whom. Decolonisation, with varied and multiple meanings, is now invoked by a variety of actors with diverse motives. This is concerning since development discourse and practice have a long history of appropriating, sanitising, and purifying progressive ideas and approaches. Historically, radical concepts and theories have been co-opted into the mainstream and appropriated by international development agencies, becoming ahistorical and apolitical in the process. Thus, critical scholars must remain vigilant so that decolonisation does not morph into a milder form of anti-racism.

Addressing these concerns and pursuing true decolonisation would require a profound transformation of development. As this book outlines, development discourse and practice are, in part, founded on colonial legacies manifest in contemporary understandings of modernity and progress. A development industry that forges distinctions and hierarchies between people and societies, places, and cultures is not well placed to forge decoloniality. Indeed, many who are currently engaged in development may need to move out of the way, vacate the space, and remain silent to allow formerly colonised, Indigenous, and marginalised people to guide debates about decolonisation and decoloniality.

Researchers, practitioners, and policy makers in and of the West need to actively acknowledge and work to address past injustices. In *Time's Place*, Tronto (2003: 119) argues that 'the privileging of the future over the past' creates problems 'for thinking about justice for historical wrongdoing'. As Raghuram et al. (2009: 10) contend, framing the past as irrelevant 'leaves no room for remedying past injustices or for moving towards a responsible accountability'. This engagement with the past must go *beyond* development's colonial history, as development's more recent past is also filled with violence: from forced sterilisation programmes for population control in the 1970s, to the power and control of participatory development, the ongoing displacement of millions of marginalised, Indigenous people to make way for large infrastructure projects, agricultural production with calamitous environmental effects, and shifting land ownership. These are all now part of the history of development.

Tuck and Yang's (2012: 2) ground-breaking work, *Decolonisation is not a Metaphor*, is again instructive. They remind us that decolonisation 'cannot easily be grafted onto pre-existing discourses/frameworks, even if they are critical, even if they are anti-racist, even if they are justice frameworks'. They warn against using decolonisation to further embed settler power and futurities, noting that 'decolonization, which we assert is a distinct project from other civil and human rights-based social justice projects, is far too often subsumed into the directives of these projects, with no regard for how decolonization wants something different than those forms of justice' (Tuck and Yang 2012: 3). Decolonisation must have material effects, including the repatriation of land and territory. The next section turns to ideas of reparations as redistributive justice.

Reparations and redistribution

Some Global South governments and communities have called for reparations to help right the wrongs of slavery, the slave trade, and colonialism. Such reparations to redress historical violence have empirical precedent. For instance, in 2003, the British government paid about £20 million in reparations to more than 5000 Kenyans who survived abuse by British colonialists during the Mau Mau rebellion in the 1950s. After World War II, Germany was ordered to pay Holocaust reparations to Polish and Jewish survivors and, in 1989, the US paid over US$1.2 billion to Japanese-Americans who were detained in internment camps (Campbell 2009). More recently, the Canadian Human Rights Tribunal decided that the Canadian federal government should pay C$40 000 to more than 150 000 people who were impacted by the systemic brutality of residential schools (Schalk 2022). This decision followed Canada's Truth and Reconciliation Commission's findings; however, the Tribunal's decision is currently being challenged by the Canadian federal government (Fouksman and Klein 2019; Klein 2023). Globally, while some reparations have been paid, many more demands remain unanswered.

In 1993, the Organisation of African Unity sponsored the Pan-African Conference on Reparations for Enslavement and Colonisation. This conference resulted in the Abuja Proclamation (1993), which called for

> the international community to recognise that there is a unique and unprecedented moral debt owed to the African peoples which has yet to be paid – the debt of compensation to the Africans as the most humiliated and exploited people of the last four centuries of modern history … [It] further urges the Organization of African Unity to call for full monetary payment of repayments through capital transfer and debt cancellation … Convinced that the claim for reparations is well grounded in International Law, it urges on the Organization of African Unity to establish a legal Committee on the issue of Reparations [… It] serves notice on all states in Europe and the Americas which had participated in the enslavement and colonisation of the African peoples, and which may still be engaged in racism and neo-colonialism, to desist from any further damage and start building bridges of conciliation, co-operation, and … reparation.

Perhaps the largest global effort to demand reparations for colonialism came from the 2001 World Conference Against Racism in Durban. The conference covered many themes, including reparations for slavery and colonisation, and resulted in an action plan to eradicate racial discrimination and intolerance through education and international cooperation. Reparations were part of a wider push to unravel structures of racism through recognition and compensation. Before many of the world's governments and their representatives convened to negotiate the final declaration, over 4000 NGOs met to collectively draft demands for reparations for 'crimes against humanity', including the trans-Atlantic slave trade, slavery, and colonisation. Some governments rejected the draft, arguing that this wording was too 'strong' (Fouksman and Klein 2019; Klein 2023).

All references to reparations for colonisation were removed from the final conference declaration. Instead, nations benefiting from the slave trade were encouraged to provide aid (Lyons 2002). Most recently, the intergovernmental organisation Caribbean Community (CARICOM) established the CARICOM Reparations Commission in 2013. It produced a Ten Point Plan calling for necessary 'payment of reparations by the former colonial European countries to the nations and people of the Caribbean Community, for Native genocide, the transatlantic slave trade and a racialised system of chattel slavery' (Beckles 2013). However, this plan has, thus far, been met with silence from Western governments.

Reparative justice has also been demanded as a form of climate justice for what is known as Loss and Damage (see Boyd et al. 2021). Loss and Damage seeks to acknowledge the extraordinary loss faced by Global South populations who are most vulnerable to the impacts of climate change, but least responsible. These inequalities are compounded by enduring structural inequalities in the global economic and political system. Negotiations for specific reparations in the Loss and Damage space are ongoing and are often met with the West's refusal to take responsibility and offer justice. Reparations for climate justice demand more than compensation. They seek to transform economic and political systems that continually undermine the lives and futures of Indigenous people and others in the Global South (Táíwò 2022; Perry 2021). According to Táíwò (2022), reparations as a means of transformation hold the promise of 'worldmaking' to reconstruct the *global racial empire* that underpins the climate crisis and racist norms, laws, and policies (Klein 2023). When reparations are granted, they are generally administered as one-off events recognised by the state and judiciary. However, reparations can also be integrated into larger redistributive systems that transform the unjust social and economic structures established during colonialism and slavery that continue to shape local and global societies and economies.

Towards pluriversality

One enduring problem with development is its obsession with linearity and universalism, which are largely based on Western ideas of progress. This results in the systematic denial of the diversity of life worlds, ontologies, economies, ecologies, and societies. Scholars, activists, and communities have long called for alternative economies to unsettle these universalising and globalising tendencies. Now, it is imperative to move beyond critiques and identify transformative alternative ways to perceive and explain the world. One such approach is pluriversality (see Escobar 2018).

Esteva, drawing on the Zapatista phrase, envisions 'a world in which many worlds can be embraced' (Esteva and Escobar 2017: 4). This shift welcomes different ways of imagining life and accepts diverse ontologies and other modes of existence (Escobar 2011). As Hutchings (2019: 115) suggests, 'instead of aiming to know the meaning of global justice and then apply it to particular contexts, a pluriversal ethics addresses the question of how to cultivate a practical ethic of coexistence and collaboration with others in an ontologically plural and radically hierarchical world'. As a political project, pluriversality raises important questions about where and by whom knowledge is produced and how it circulates (Agnew and Livingstone 2011). The pluriverse fundamentally challenges the imposition of Western universalist claims about humanity (i.e. Mignolo's, 2011, ongoing 'colonial matrix of power'; see also Quijano 2007).

Pluriversality understands that there 'are worlds out there (and always have been) that have historically been marginalized and suppressed by a Western cosmology and universalizing tendency that claimed a superior position for itself vis-à-vis those "other" worlds' (Oslender 2019: 1693). The concept, therefore, emerged from the decolonial desire to challenge this dominance and to strive towards the 'entanglement of diverse cosmologies, of which Western universalism is but one' (Oslender 2019: 1693). This requires interrogating colonial legacies in contemporary forms of knowledge and, as Reiter (2018: 2) suggests, actively constructing a pluriverse to move beyond 'one-dimensional solutions to diverse problems'.

The pluriverse is now a central tenet of decolonial thinking, inspired in large part by 'Indigenous movements in Latin America and elsewhere that have resisted the encroachments of modernity in the form of industrialisation, urbanisation, and ecological devastation' (Hutchings 2019: 115). As Mignolo (2018: ix) suggests, 'it was the Zapatistas' own decolonial political vision of a world in which many worlds would coexist that announced the pluriverse'. The Zapatistas and other activist movements see themselves as located in radically different worlds that offer alternative places and times from which to mobilise resistance to modernity (Hutchings 2019: 115).

The recognition that there is no single Western world, but multiple worlds with varied environmental, social, economic, and political contexts serves as a fundamental distinction between Western, colonial modernity and other ways of being. Additionally, pluriversal possibilities for lives and livelihoods are disconnected from processes of capital accumulation and support flourishing alternatives to capitalism (Escobar 2011). The pluriverse critiques Eurocentric claims to universality by asserting multiple ontologies (Hutchings 2019: 116) and offering alternatives to Western modernity and capitalism. The pluriverse makes 'alternatives to one world plausible to one-worlders' and 'provide[s] resonance to those other worlds that interrupt the one world story' (Escobar 2019: 50). These other worlds hold the possibility for developing alternative ontologies with less devastating effects.

Disrupting hegemonic one-world stories is not easy; the relations between different worlds are founded on hierarchies and inequalities. Kothari et al. (2019: xxxv) acknowledge the challenge of building synergies across different worlds but are optimistic that differences, tensions, contradictions, and conflicts 'can become a basis for constructive exchange'. They explain 'what has been missing is a broad transcultural compilation of concrete concepts, worldviews, and practices from around the world, challenging the modernist ontology of universalism in favour of a multiplicity of possible worlds. This is what it means to call for a pluriverse'. Similarly, Gills and Hosseini (2022: 1186–7) ask:

> how to co-develop an inclusive and dynamic knowledge of the pluriverse of transformative alternatives and to make this knowledge a historical force that actively empowers and synergizes myriad transformational actors and strengthens their practices. … ambitious and 'utopian' visions … [such that] alternatives appear as not just ideas and imaginations but also lived experiences, creative works, and social practices.

While much theoretical and conceptual work has been done on pluriver-sality, there remains a dearth of ethnographic evidence documenting the actually existing pluriverse (Oslender 2019). This is not due to an absence of alternatives to colonial modernity. Indeed, different worlds are already present at many sites where 'border thinking' (Mignolo 2011) is being advanced. Some of this pluriversal diversity is well-known, such as *Buen Vivir* in South America and *ubuntu* in southern Africa. Other examples are based on alternative political visions like eco-socialism, degrowth, and ecofeminism (Kothari et al., 2019). Gibson-Graham's (2006: 60) com-munity economies approach reclaims the diversity of economies beyond capitalism and identifies 'all of those practices excluded or marginalized by a strong theory of capitalism'. Gibson-Graham recognises the inter-dependence of a broad range of economic and so-called *noneconomic* activities. These include practices of unpaid care, community-based communing, solidarity projects and local support groups. Many of these existing alternatives simply need more space to flourish.

This book has reviewed ideas and concepts that aid in the critical rethink-ing of development. Such critiques fundamentally question the problem-atic foundations of development, including unequal spatial and temporal classifications; forms of exclusion and inclusion; structures, processes, and goals of uneven development; narratives that dispossess; representa-tions that reinforce hierarchical distinctions; and development designs and measurements that conceal more than they reveal. It is imperative to get beyond the singular, unilinear framings of development.

Questions remain about what solidarity, decoloniality and pluriversality mean for the field of development, which has long tried to sidestep its history. However, critical development scholars are beginning to create spaces for new ways of thinking to emerge that draw on Indigenous trans-formative ideas and practices.

References

Abrahamsen, R. (2012). 'Security privatization and the new contours of Africa's security governance', in Cornelissen, S., Cheru, F. and Shaw, T.M. (eds.) *Africa and international relations in the 21st century*. London: Palgrave Macmillan, pp. 162–176.

Acemoglu, D., Simon, J. and James, A.R. (2001). 'The colonial origins of comparative development: an empirical investigation', *American Economic Review*, 91(5), pp. 1369–1401.

Achebe, C. (1958). *Things fall apart*. New York: Anchor.

Adams, W.B. (2019). *Green development: Environment and sustainability in a developing world*. London: Routledge.

Adams, W.M. and Mulligan, M. (eds.) (2002). *Decolonizing nature: strategies for conservation in a post-colonial era*. London: Routledge.

Adey, P., Hannam, K., Sheller, M. and Typfield, D. (2021). 'Pandemic (im)mobilities', *Mobilities*, 16(1), pp. 1–19.

Agarwal, B. (1997). '"Bargaining" and gender relations: within and beyond the household', *Feminist Economics*, 3(1), pp. 1–51.

Aghajanian, A. and Allouche, J. (2016). 'Introduction: development studies – past, present and future', *IDS Bulletin*, 47(2), pp. 1–12.

Agnew, J. and Livingstone, D. (2011). 'Introduction', in Agnew, J. and Livingstone, D. (eds.) *The Sage handbook of geographical knowledge*. Thousand Oaks, CA: Sage, pp. 1–17.

Ahmad, A. (1995). 'The politics of literary postcoloniality', *Race & Class*, 36(3), pp. 1–20.

Ahmed, S. (2017). *Living a feminist life*. Durham, NC: Duke University Press.

Allan, J. (2007). *Rethinking inclusive education*. Dordrecht: Springer.

Amin, S. (1976). *Unequal development: an essay on the social formations of peripheral capitalism*. Translated by P. Brian. New York: Monthly Review Press.

Anthias, F. (2012). 'Transnational mobilities, migration research and intersectionality', *Nordic Journal of Migration Research*, 2(2), pp. 102–110.

Anthias, F. (2013). 'Intersectional what? Social divisions, intersectionality and levels of analysis', *Ethnicities*, 13(1), pp. 3–19.

Appadurai, A. (1990). 'Disjuncture and difference in the global cultural economy', in Featherstone, M. (ed.) *Global culture*. London: Sage, pp. 295–310.

Artur, L. and Hilhorst, D. (2012). 'Everyday realities of climate change adaptation in Mozambique', *Global Environmental Change*, 22(2), pp. 529–536.

Austin, L. and Frize, J. (2011). *Ready or not? Emergency cash transfers at scale*. Oxford: CALP Network. Available at: http://www.cashlearning.org/downloads/

resources/calp/CaLP%20Ready%20Or%20Not%20-%20Emergency%20Cash%20Transfers%20At%20Scale.pdf (accessed: 9 August 2017).

Bakewell, O. (2011). 'Conceptualising displacement and migration: processes, conditions, and categories', in Koser, K. and Martin, S. (eds.) *The migration-displacement nexus: Patterns, processes, and policies.* New York: Berghahn, pp. 14–28.

Baldwin, J. (2007). *No name in the street.* New York: Vintage Books.

Baldwin, R. (2016). *The great convergence: Information technology and the new globalization.* Cambridge, MA: Harvard University Press.

Ball, J. (2014). 'Children learn better in the mother tongue', *Global Partnership*, 21 February. Available at: https://www.globalpartnership.org/blog/children-learn-better-their-mother-tongue (accessed: 14 February 2023).

Barker, F., Hulme, P. and Iversen, M. (eds.) (1994). *Colonial discourse and postcolonial theory.* Manchester: Manchester University Press.

Barnett, M. and Weiss, T.G. (eds.) (2008). *Humanitarianism in question: politics, power, ethics.* Ithaca, NY: Cornell University Press.

Basic Income Earth Network. (n.d.). *BIEN.* Available at: https://basicincome.org (accessed: 20 October 2022).

Bastia, T. (2014). 'Intersectionality, migration and development', *Progress in Development Studies*, 14(3), pp. 237–248.

Bastia, T., Lulle, A. and King, R. (2022). 'Migration and development: the overlooked roles of older people and ageing', *Progress in Human Geography*, 46(4), pp. 1009–1027.

Bastia, T. and Skeldon, R. (eds.) (2020). *Routledge handbook of migration and development.* London: Routledge.

Bauer, P.T. (1984). *Reality and rhetoric: studies in the economics of development.* London: Weidenfield & Nicolson.

Bebbington, A.J. and Batterbury, S.P. (2001). 'Transnational livelihoods and landscapes: political ecologies of globalization', *Ecumene*, 8(4), pp. 369–380.

Beckles, H. (2013). *Britain's Black debt: reparations for Caribbean slavery and native genocide.* Kingston: University of the West Indies Press.

Benhabib, S. (2007). 'Twilight of sovereignty or the emergence of cosmopolitan norms? Rethinking citizenship in volatile times', *Citizenship Studies*, 11(1), pp. 19–36.

Benyera, E. (2022). *The failure of the international criminal court in Africa: decolonising global justice.* London: Routledge.

Bernards, N. (2017). 'The global governance of informal economies: the international labour organization in East Africa', *Third World Quarterly*, 38(8), pp. 1831–1846.

Beymer-Farris, B.A. and Bassett, T.J. (2012). 'The REDD menace: resurgent protectionism in Tanzania's mangrove forests', *Global Environmental Change*, 22(2), pp. 332–341.

Bhabha, H. (1984). 'Of mimicry and man: the ambivalence of colonial discourse', *Discipleship*, 28, pp. 125–133.

Bhattacharyya, G. (2018). *Rethinking racial capitalism: questions of reproduction and survival.* London: Rowman and Littlefield.

Birn, A.-E., Pillay, Y. and Holtz, T.H. (2009). *Textbook of international health: global health in a dynamic world.* 3rd edn. Oxford: Oxford University Press.

Black, R., Collyer, M., Skeldon, R. and Waddington, C. (2006). 'Routes to illegal residence: a case study of immigration detainees in the United Kingdom', *Geoforum*, 37(4), pp. 552–564.

Blaikie, P. and Brookfield, H. (1987). *Land degradation and society*. London: Routledge.

Boillat, S. and Berkes, F. (2013). 'Perception and interpretation of climate change among Quechua farmers of Bolivia: Indigenous knowledge as a resource for adaptive capacity', *Ecology and Society*, 18(4), p. 21.

Boltanski, L. (1999). *Distant suffering: morality, media and politics*. Translated by G.D. Burchell. Cambridge: Cambridge University Press.

Bond, P. and Dor, G. (2003). 'Uneven health outcomes and political resistance under residual neoliberalism in Africa', *International Journal of Health Services*, 33(3), pp. 607–630.

Borda-Rodriguez, A. and Lanfranco, S. (2011). 'Knowledge and technology for development', in Henry, V. (ed.) *The critical development studies handbook: tools for change*. Halifax: Fernwood Publishing, pp. 160–165.

Boyd, E., Chaffin, B.C., Dorkenoo, K., Jackson, G., Harrington, L., N'Guetta, A., Johansson, E.L., Nordlander, L., De Rosa, S. P., Raju, E., Scown, M., Soo, J. and Stuart-Smith, R. (2021). 'Loss and damage from climate change: a new climate justice agenda', *One Earth*, 4(10), pp. 1365–1370.

Bozorgmehr, K. (2010). 'Rethinking the "global" in global health: a dialectic approach', *Globalization and Health*, 6(1), pp. 1–19.

Briggs, J. and Sharp, J. (2004). 'Indigenous knowledges and development: a postcolonial caution', *Third World Quarterly*, 25(4), pp. 661–676.

Brockington, D. (2014). *Celebrity advocacy and international development*. London: Routledge.

Brohman, J. (1995). 'Universalism, eurocentrism, and ideological bias in development studies: from modernisation to neoliberalism', *Third World Quarterly*, 16(1), pp. 121–140.

Brundtland, G.H. (1987). *Report of the World Commission on environment and development: 'our common future'*. New York: United Nations.

Bryant, R.L. (1998). 'Power, knowledge and political ecology in the Third World: a review', *Progress in Physical Geography*, 22(1), pp. 79–94.

Bryant, R.L. (2015). 'Reflecting on political ecology', in Bryant, R.L. (ed.) *The international handbook of political ecology*. Cheltenham, UK, and Northampton, MA: Edward Elgar Publishing, pp. 14–26.

Buffett, P. (2013). 'The charitable–industrial complex', *New York Times*, 26 July. Available at: http://www.coloradoinclusivefunders.org/uploads/1/1/5/0/11506731/the_charitable-industrial_complex_-_nytimes_com.pdf (accessed: 5 May 2022).

Burman, E. (2007). *Developments: child, image, nation*. London: Routledge.

Büscher, B. (2019). 'From "global" to "revolutionary" development', *Development and Change*, 50(2), pp. 484–494.

Buse, K. and Walt, G. (2000). 'Policy and practice global public–private partnerships: part I – a new development in health?', *Bulletin of the World Health Organization*, 78(99), pp. 549–561.

Butler, J. (2015). *Notes toward a performative theory of assembly*. Cambridge, MA: Harvard University Press.

Campbell, D. (2011). 'The iconography of famine', in Batchen, G., Gidley, M., Miller, N. K. and Prosser, J. (eds) *Picturing atrocity: photography in crisis*. Chicago: University of Chicago Press, pp. 79–92.

Campbell, J.T. (2009). 'Settling accounts? An Americanist perspective on historical reconciliation', *American Historical Review*, 114(4), pp. 963–977.

Cannon, K.L. (2014). 'Anti-poverty policy as the cultivation of market subjects: the case of the conditional cash transfer program Oportunidades', Master's thesis, University of Ottawa, Canada.

Caretta, M.A. and Morgan, R. (2021). 'Special issue on Indigenous knowledge for water-related climate adaptation', *Climate and Development*, 13(9), pp. 761–765.

Carpio, G., Barnd, N.B. and Barraclough, L. (2022). 'Introduction to the special issue: mobilizing indigeneity and race within and against settler colonialism', *Mobilities*, 17(2), pp. 179–195.

Castells, M. (1996). *The rise of the network society*. Vol. 1. Oxford: Blackwell.

Castree, N. (1995). 'The nature of produced nature: Materiality and knowledge construction in Marxism', *Antipode*, 27(1), pp. 12–12.

Chambers, R. (1992). *Rural appraisal: rapid, relaxed, and participatory*. IDS Discussion Paper 311. Sussex: Institute of Development Studies.

Chambers, R. (1997). *Whose reality counts? Putting the first last*. London: IT Publications.

Chant, S. (1998). 'Households, gender and rural–urban migration: reflections on linkages and considerations for policy', *Environment and Urbanization*, 10(1), pp. 5–22.

Chatterjee, P. (2008). 'Democracy and economic transformation in India', *Economic & Political Weekly*, 43(16), pp. 53–62.

Cheeseman, N., Death, C. and Whitfield, L. (2017). 'Notes on researching Africa', *African Affairs*, 121(485), pp. e87–e91.

Chen, M. (2012). *The informal economy: definitions, theories and policies*. WIEGO Working Paper No. 1. Available at: http://wiego.org/publications/informal-economy-definitions-theories-and-policies (accessed: 10 January 2017).

Chouliaraki, L. (2011). '"Improper distance": towards a critical account of solidarity as irony', *International Journal of Cultural Studies*, 14(4), pp. 363–381.

Chouliaraki, L. (2013). *The ironic spectator: solidarity in the age of post-humanitarianism*. Cambridge: Polity Press.

Chuji, M., Rengifo, G. and Gudynas, E. (2019). '*Buen Vivir*', in Kothari, A., Salleh, A., Escobar, A., Demaria, F. and Acosta, A. (eds.) *Pluriverse: a post-development dictionary*. New Delhi: Tulika Books, pp. 111–114.

Clay, N. and King, B. (2019). 'Smallholders' uneven capacities to adapt to climate change amid Africa's "green revolution": case study of Rwanda's crop intensification program', *World Development*, 116, pp. 1–14.

Cleaver, H.M. (1972). 'The contradictions of the green revolution', *American Economic Review*, 62(1/2), pp. 177–186.

Cochran, P., Huntington, O.H., Pungowiyi, C., Tom, S., Chapin III, F.S., Huntington, H.P., Maynard, N.G. and Trainor, S.F. (2014). 'Indigenous frameworks for observing and responding to climate change in Alaska', in Koppel Maldonado, J., Colombi, B. and Pandya, R. (eds.) *Climate change and Indigenous peoples in the United States*. Amsterdam: Springer, pp. 49–59.

Cohen, B.J. (1973). *The question of imperialism: the political economy of dominance and dependence.* New York: Basic Books.

Collins, P.H. (2015). 'Intersectionality's definitional dilemmas', *Annual Review of Sociology*, 41(1), pp. 1–20.

Comaroff, J. and Comaroff, J.L. (2012). *Theory from the south: or, how Euro-America is evolving toward Africa.* London: Routledge.

Cooke, B. (2003). 'A new continuity with colonial administration: participation in development management', *Third World Quarterly*, 24(1), pp. 47–61.

Cooke, B. and Kothari, U. (eds.) (2001). *Participation: the new tyranny?* London: Zed Books.

Cornia, A., Jolly, R., Stewart, F. and UNICEF. (eds.) (1987). *Adjustment with a human face: protecting the vulnerable and promoting growth.* Oxford: Clarendon Press. Available at: https://digitallibrary.un.org/record/46296?ln=en (accessed: 19 January 2021).

Coulthard, G.S. (2014). *Red skin, white masks: rejecting the colonial politics of recognition.* Minneapolis: University of Minnesota Press.

Cowen, M. and Shenton, R.W. (eds.) (1996). 'The invention of development', in Crush, J. (ed.) *Power of development.* London: Routledge, pp. 3–21.

Cresswell, T. (2010). 'Towards a politics of mobility', *Environment and Planning D: Society and Space*, 28(1), pp. 17–31.

Cresswell, T. (2014). 'Mobilities III: moving on', *Progress in Human Geography*, 38(5), pp. 712–721.

Cresswell, T. (2021). 'Valuing mobility in a post COVID-19 world', *Mobilities*, 16(1), pp. 51–65

Crush, J. (ed.) (1995). *Power of development.* London: Routledge.

Crush, J. and Chikanda, A. (2018). 'Staunching the flow: the brain drain and health professional retention strategies in South Africa', in Czaika, M. (ed.) *High-skilled migration: drivers and policies.* Oxford: Oxford University Press, pp. 337–359.

Cueto, M. (2004). 'The origins of primary health care and selective primary health care', *American Journal of Public Health*, 94(11), pp. 1864–1874.

Cueto, M. (2013). 'A return to the magic bullet? Malaria and global health in the twenty-first century', in Biehl, J. and Petryna, A. (eds.) *When people come first: critical studies in global health.* Princeton, NJ: Princeton University Press, pp. 30–53.

Currie-Alder, B. (2016). 'The state of development studies: origins, evolution and prospects', *Canadian Journal of Development Studies/Revue canadienne d'études du développement*, 37(1), pp. 5–26.

D'Costa, A. (2014). 'Compressed capitalism and development: primitive accumulation, petty commodity production, and capitalist maturity in India and China', *Critical Asian Studies*, 46(2), pp. 317–344.

Davala, S., Jhabvala, R., Standing, G. and Mehta, S.K. (2015). *Basic income: a transformative policy for India.* London: Bloomsbury Publishing.

De Brauw, A., Gilligan, D.O., Hoddinott, J. and Roy, S. (2014). 'The impact of Bolsa Família on women's decision-making power', *World Development*, 59, pp. 487–504.

De Haas, H. (2010). 'Migration and development: a theoretical perspective', *International Migration Review*, 44(1), pp. 227–264.

Delgado Wise, R. and Márquez Covarrubias, H. (2009). 'Understanding the relationship between migration and development', *Social Analysis*, 53(3), pp. 85–105.

Demaria, F. and Kothari, A. (2017). 'The post-development dictionary agenda: paths to the pluriverse', *Third World Quarterly*, 38(12), pp. 2588–2599.

Dengler, C. and Seebacher, L.M. (2019). 'What about the Global South? Towards a feminist decolonial degrowth approach', *Ecological Economics*, 157, pp. 246–252.

Digital History. (2021). *Migration as a key theme in U.S. and world history.* Available at: http://www.digitalhistory.uh.edu/disp_textbook.cfm?smtID=2& psid=3300 (accessed: 14 February 2023).

Dirks, N. (1992). *Colonialism and culture.* Ann Arbor: University of Michigan Press.

Dos Santos, T. (1973). 'The crisis of development theory and the problem of dependence in Latin America', in Bernstein, H. (ed.) *Underdevelopment and development: the Third World today.* Baltimore: Penguin Books, pp. 57–71.

Douzinas, C. (2000). *The end of human rights: critical legal thought at the turn of century.* Oxford: Hart Publishing.

Drissi, S. (2020). 'Indigenous peoples and the nature they protect', *Nature Action UNEP*, 8 June. Available at: https://www.unep.org/news-and-stories/story/ indigenous-peoples-and-nature-they-protect (accessed: 27 October 2022).

Du Bois, W.E.B. (2015 [1903]). *The souls of Black folk.* London: Routledge.

Edensor, T., Head, L. and Kothari, U. (2019). 'Time, temporality and environmental change', *Geoforum*, 108, pp. 255–258.

Elson, D. (ed.) (1995). *Male bias in the development process.* 2nd edn. Manchester: Manchester University Press.

Engle-Merry, S. (2011). 'Measuring the world: indicators, human rights, and global governance', *Current Anthropology*, 52(S3), pp. S83–S95.

Escobar, A. (1988). 'Power and visibility: development and the invention and management of the Third World', *Cultural Anthropology*, 3(4), pp. 428–443.

Escobar, A. (1995). *Encountering development: the making and unmaking of the Third World.* Princeton, NJ: Princeton University Press.

Escobar, A. (2011). *Encountering development: The making and unmaking of the Third World* (Vol. 1). Princeton: Princeton University Press.

Escobar, A. (2018). *Designs for the pluriverse: radical interdependence, autonomy, and the making of worlds.* Durham, NC: Duke University Press.

Escobar, A. (2019). 'Thinking-feeling with the Earth: territorial struggles and the ontological dimension of the epistemologies of the south', in *Knowledges born in the struggle.* London: Routledge, pp. 41–57.

Esson, J., Noxolo, P., Baxter, R., Daley, P and Byron, M. (2017). 'The 2017 RGS-IBG chair's theme: decolonising geographical knowledges, or reproducing coloniality?', *Area*, 49(3), pp. 384–388.

Esteva, G. and Escobar, A. (2017). 'Post-development @ 25: on "being stuck" and moving forward, sideways, backward and otherwise', *Third World Quarterly*, 38(12), pp. 2559–2572.

Eyben, R. (2012). 'The hegemony cracked: the power guide to getting care onto the development agenda', *IDS Working Papers*, 2012(411), pp. 1–29.

Faist, T. (2007). 'Migrants as transnational development agents: an inquiry into the newest round of the migration–development nexus', *Population, Space and Place*, 14(1), pp. 21–42.

Fantom, N. and Serajuddin, U. (2016). *The World Bank's classification of countries by income*. World Bank Policy Research Working Paper No. 7528.

Farmer, P., Kleinman, A., Kim, J.Y. and Basilico, M. (2013). *Reimagining global health: an introduction*. Berkeley: University of California Press.

Fassin, D. (2017). 'The endurance of critique', *Anthropological Theory*, 17(1), pp. 4–29.

Faulconbridge, J. and Hui, A. (2016). 'Traces of a mobile field: ten years of mobilities research', *Mobilities*, 11(1), pp. 1–14.

Favell, A. (2022). 'The state of migration theory: challenges, interdisciplinarity, and critique', in *Migration theory*. 2nd edn. London: Routledge, pp. 341–358.

Featherstone, D. (2012). *Solidarity: hidden histories and geographies of internationalism*. London: Zed Books.

Federici, S. (2012). *Revolution at point zero: housework, reproduction, and feminist struggle*. Oakland, CA: PM Press.

Ferguson, J. (1990). *The anti-politics machine: 'development', depolitisation and bureaucratic power in Lesotho*. Minneapolis: University of Minnesota Press.

Ferguson, J. (2015). *Give a man a fish: reflections on the new politics of distribution*. Durham, NC: Duke University Press.

Ferguson, J. (2017). 'Author's response', *Antipode Online*, 1 February. Available at: https://antipodeonline.org/2017/02/01/give-a-man-a-fish/ (accessed: 22 October 2022).

Fiddian-Qasmiyeh, E. (2020). 'Introduction: recentering the South in studies of migration', *Migration and Society*, 3(1), pp. 1–18.

Fiszbein, A. and Schady, N.R. (2009). *Conditional cash transfers: reducing present and future poverty*. Washington, DC: World Bank Publications.

Fofana, M.O. (2021). 'Decolonising global health in the time of COVID-19', *Global Public Health*, 16(8–9), pp. 1155–1166.

Folbre, N. (2012). 'Valuing care', in *For love and money: care provision in the United States*. New York: Russell Sage Foundation, pp. 92–111.

Ford, J.D., Cameron, L., Rubis, J., Maillet, M., Nakashima, D., Willox, A.C. and Pearce, T. (2016). 'Including Indigenous knowledge and experience in IPCC assessment reports', *Nature Climate Change*, 6, pp. 349–353.

Fort, M., Mercer, M. and Gish, O. (eds.) (2004). *Sickness and wealth: the corporate assault on health*. Cambridge: South End Press.

Fortier, A.M. (2014). 'Migration studies', in Adey, P., Bissell, D., Hannam, K., Merriman, P. and Sheller, M. (eds.) *The Routledge handbook of mobilities*. London: Routledge, pp. 64–73.

Fouksman, E. and Klein, E. (2019). 'Radical transformation or technological intervention? Two paths for universal basic income', *World Development*, 122, pp. 492–500.

Frank, A.G. (1966). *The development of underdevelopment*. Boston: New England Free Press.

Frankel, B. (2018). *Fictions of sustainability: the politics of growth and post-capitalist futures*. Melbourne: Greenmeadows.

Fraser, N. (2016). 'Contradictions of capital and care', *New Left Review*, 100, pp. 1–34.

Freire, P. (1970). 'Cultural action and conscientization', *Harvard Educational Review*, 40(3), pp. 452–477.

Freire, P. (2018 [1968]). *Pedagogy of the oppressed*. New York: Bloomsbury Publishing.

Friedman, M. (1953). *Essays in positive economics*. Chicago: University of Chicago Press.

Galien, C. (2020). 'A decolonial turn in the humanities', *Alif: Journal of Comparative Poetics*, 40, pp. 28–58

Gao, Q. and Hopkins, P. (2022). 'Using intersectionality to explore social inequalities amongst Christian family migrants in China', *The Geographical Journal*, 188(2), pp. 177–189.

Getachew, A. (2019). *Worldmaking after empire: the rise and fall of self-determination*. Princeton, NJ: Princeton University Press.

Gibson, C. and Warren, A. (2020). 'Keeping time with trees: climate change, forest resources, and experimental relations with the future', *Geoforum*, 108, pp. 325–337.

Gibson-Graham, J.K. (2006). *A postcapitalist politics*. Minneapolis: University of Minnesota Press.

Gillespie, T. (2016). 'Accumulation by urban dispossession: struggles over urban space in Accra, Ghana', *Transactions of the Institute of British Geographers*, 41(1), pp. 66–77.

Gills, B.K. and Hosseini, S.A.H. (2022). 'Pluriversality and beyond: consolidating radical alternatives to (mal-) development as a communist project', *Sustainability Science*, 17, pp. 1183–1194.

Glick Shiller, N., Basch, L. and Szanton Blanc, C. (1995). 'From immigrant to transmigrant: theorizing transnational migration', *Anthropological Quarterly*, 68(1), pp. 48–63.

Global Development Studies. (2018). *Description of the Discipline*. Global Development Studies, University of Helsinki. Available at: https://blogs.helsinki.fi/developmentstudies/2018/09/26/description-of-the-discipline/ (accessed: 10 January 2022).

Godlewska, A. and Smith, N. (1994). *Geography and empire*. Oxford: Blackwell.

Goldsmith, E. (1997). 'Development as colonialism', *The Ecologist*, 27(1), p. 69.

Goodyear-Ka'ōpua, N. (2013). *The seeds we planted: portraits of a native Hawaiian charter school*. Minneapolis: University of Minnesota Press.

Gordon, L.R. and Gordon, J.A. (2015). *Not only the master's tools: African American studies in theory and practice*. London: Routledge.

Gray, K. and Gills, B.K. (2016). 'South–South cooperation and the rise of the Global South', *Third World Quarterly*, 37(4), pp. 557–574.

Gray, K. and Murphy, C.N. (2013). 'Introduction: rising powers and the future of global governance', *Third World Quarterly*, 34(2), pp. 183–193.

Greer, S. (2014). 'Structural adjustment comes to Europe: lessons for the Eurozone from the conditionality debates', *Global Social Policy*, 14(1), pp. 51–71.

Griffiths, I. (1986). 'The scramble for Africa: inherited political boundaries', *The Geographical Journal*, 152(2), pp. 204–216.

Grillo, R.D. and Stirrat, R.L. (eds.) (1997). *Discourses of development: anthropological perspectives*. London: Routledge.

Grosfoguel, R. (2007). 'The epistemic decolonial turn: beyond political-economy paradigms', *Cultural Studies*, 21(2–3), pp. 211–223.

Grosfoguel, R. (2011). 'Decolonizing post-colonial studies and paradigms of political-economy: transmodernity, decolonial thinking, and global coloniality', *TRANSMODERNITY: Journal of Peripheral Cultural Production of the Luso-Hispanic World*, 1(1).

Grosfoguel, R., Oso, L. and Christou, A. (2015). '"Racism", intersectionality and migration studies: framing some theoretical reflections', *Identities*, 22(6), pp. 635–652.

Guijt, I. and Shah, M. (1998). *The myth of community: gender issues in participatory development*. London: IT Publications.

Haarmann, C., Haarmann, D., Jauch, H., Shindondola-Mote, H., Nattrass, N., van Niekerk, I. and Samson, M. (2009). *Making the difference! The BIG in Namibia: basic income grant pilot project assessment report*. Windhoek, Namibia: NANGOF. Available at: http://www.bignam.org/Publications/BIG_Assessment_report_08b.pdf (accessed: 10 August 2017).

Hage, G. (2012). 'Critical anthropological thought and the radical political imaginary today', *Critique of Anthropology*, 32(3), pp. 285–308.

Hage, G. (2017). *Is racism an environmental threat?* Hoboken, NJ: John Wiley & Sons.

Hall, C. (2009). 'Macaulay's nation', *Victorian Studies*, 51(3), pp. 505–523.

Hall, S. (1980). 'Race, articulation and societies structured in dominance', in United Nations Education and Cultural Organization (ed.) *Sociological theories: race and colonialism*. Paris: UNESCO, pp. 305–345.

Hall, S. (ed.) (1997). *Representation: cultural representations and signifying practices*. Thousand Oaks, CA: Sage.

Hall, S. and Gieben, B. (1992). 'The West and the rest: discourse and power', in Das Gupta, T., James, C.E., Andersen, C., Galabuzi, G.-E. and Maaka, R.C.A. (eds.) *Race and racialization*. 2nd end. Toronto: Canadian Scholars' Press, pp. 85–95.

Halttunen, K. (1995). 'Humanitarianism and the pornography of pain in Anglo-American culture', *American Historical Review*, 100(2), pp. 303–334.

Hammar, T., Brochmann, G., Tamas, K. and Faist, T. (eds.) (2021). *International migration, immobility and development: multidisciplinary perspectives*. London: Routledge.

Hanaček, K., Roy, B., Avila, S. and Kallis, G. (2020). 'Ecological economics and degrowth: proposing a future research agenda from the margins', *Ecological Economics*, 169, pp. 106495.

Haneef, C., Roy, B., Avila, S. and Kallis, G. (2014). *CLP's influence on dowry and violence against women on the chars*. Bogura, Bangladesh: CLP. Available at: https://assets.publishing.service.gov.uk/media/57a089cce5274a27b2000285/CLPs-influence-on-dowry-and-violence.pdf (accessed: 13 June 2016).

Hanlon, J., Barrientos, A. and Hulme, D. (2012). *Just give money to the poor: the development revolution from the GLOBAL SOUTH*. Boulder, CO: Kumarian Press.

Hannam, K., Sheller, M. and Urry, J. (2006). 'Editorial: mobilities, immobilities and moorings', *Mobilities*, 1(1), 1–22.

Harcourt, W. (2009). *Body politics in development: critical debates in gender and development*. London: Zed Books.

Harcourt, W. and Nelson, I.L. (eds.) (2015). *Practising feminist political ecologies: moving beyond the 'green economy'*. London: Zed Books.

Harding, S. (2016). 'Latin American decolonial social studies of scientific knowledge', *Science, Technology, & Human Values*, 41(6), pp. 1063–1087.

Harriss-White, B. (2006). 'Poverty and capitalism', *Economic and Political Weekly*, 41(13), pp. 1241–1246.

Hart, G. (2001). 'Development critiques in the 1990s: cul de sac and promising paths', *Progress in Human Geography*, 25(4), pp. 649–658.

Hart, G. (2010). 'D/developments after the meltdown', *Antipode*, 41(S1), pp. 117–141.

Harvey, D. (1989). *The condition of postmodernity: an enquiry into the origins of cultural change*. Hoboken, NJ: Wiley-Blackwell.

Harvey, D. (2003). *The new imperialism*. New York: Oxford University Press.

Harvey, D. (2005). *A brief history of neoliberalism*. Oxford: Oxford University Press.

Hayek, F.A. (1941). *The pure theory of capital*. Chicago: University of Chicago Press.

Head, L. (2016). *Hope and grief in the Anthropocene: re-conceptualising human–nature relations*. London: Routledge.

Herbst, J. (1990). 'The structural adjustment of politics in Africa', *World Development*, 18(7), pp. 949–958.

Hermann, C. (2017). 'Another "lost decade"? Crisis and structural adjustment in Europe and Latin America', *Globalizations*, 14(4), pp. 519–534.

Hernández, C., Perales, H. and Jaffee, D. (2020). 'Without food there is no resistance: the impact of the Zapatista conflict on agrobiodiversity and seed sovereignty in Chiapas, Mexico', *Geoforum*, 128, pp. 236–250.

Hettne, B. (1995). *Development theory and the three worlds: towards an international political economy of development*. Hoboken, NJ: Wiley.

Heyneman, S.P. (2003). 'The history and problems in the making of education policy at the World Bank 1960–2000', *International Journal of Educational Development*, 23(3), pp. 315–337.

Hickel, J. (2019a). 'Bill Gates says poverty is decreasing. He couldn't be more wrong', *The Guardian*, 29 January. Available at: https://www.theguardian.com/commentisfree/2019/jan/29/bill-gates-davos-global-poverty-infographic-neoliberal (accessed: 24 August 2022).

Hickel, J. (2019b). 'Is it possible to achieve a good life for all within planetary boundaries?', *Third World Quarterly*, 40(1), pp. 18–35.

Hickel, J. (2020). 'What does degrowth mean? A few points of clarification', *Globalizations*, 18(7), pp. 1105–1111.

Himmelweit, S. (2007). 'The prospects for caring: economic theory and policy analysis', *Cambridge Journal of Economics*, 31(4), pp. 581–599.

Holbraad, M. (2013). 'Turning a corner', *HAU: Journal of Ethnographic Theory*, 3(3), pp. 469–471

hooks, b. (1992). *Black looks: race and representation*. Boston: South End Press.

hooks, b. (1994). *Teaching to transgress: education as the practice of freedom*. New York: Routledge.

Hope, J., Freeman, C., Maclean, K., Pande, R. and Sou, G. (2021). 'Shifts to global development: is this a reframing of power, agency, and progress?', *Area*, 54(2), pp. 154–158.

Horner, R. (2020). 'Towards a new paradigm of global development? Beyond the limits of international development', *Progress in Human Geography*, 44(3), pp. 415–436.

Horner, R. (2022). 'Beyond rebranding from international to global? Lessons from geographies of global health for global development', *Area*, 54(2), pp. 159–167.

Horner, R. and Hulme, D. (2019). 'From international to global development: new geographies of 21st-century development', *Development and Change*, 50(2), pp. 347–378.

Hughes, C., Bolis, M., Fries, R. and Finigan, S. (2015). 'Women's economic inequality and domestic violence: exploring the links and empowering women', *Gender & Development*, 23(2), pp. 279–297.

Hulme, M. (2008). 'Geographical work at the boundaries of climate change', *Transactions of the Institute of British Geographers*, 33(1), pp. 5–11.

Hutchings, K. (2019). 'Decolonizing global ethics: thinking with the pluriverse', *Ethics & International Affairs*, 33(2), pp. 115–125.

Ibrahim, Y. (2015). 'Instagramming life: banal imaging and the poetics of the everyday', *Journal of Media Practice*, 16(1), pp. 42–54.

Igwe, I.O.C. (2018). 'History of the international economy: the Bretton Woods system and its impact on the economic development of developing countries', *Athens Journal of Law*, 4(2), pp. 105–126.

Intergovernmental Panel on Climate Change. (2007). *Climate Change 2007: Synthesis Report. Contribution of Working Groups I, II and III to the Fourth Assessment Report of the IPCC*. Geneva: IPCC.

International Labour Organization (ILO). (2016). *Women at work trends 2016*. Geneva: ILO. Available at: http://www.ilo.org/gender/Informationresources/Publications/WCMS_457317/lang--en/index.htm (accessed: 27 January 2017).

International Organization for Migration. (2019). *Key migration terms*. Geneva: IMO. Available at: https://www.iom.int/key-migration-terms (accessed: 12 May 2022).

International Social Science Council. (2016). *World social science report. Challenging inequalities: pathways to a just world*. Paris: UNESCO Publishing.

Jarosz, L. (1992). 'Constructing the dark continent: metaphor as geographic representation of Africa', *Geografiska Annaler: Series B, Human Geography*, 74(2), pp. 105–115.

Jepson, N. (2020). *In China's wake: how the commodity boom transformed development strategies in the Global South*. New York: Columbia University Press.

Jolly, R. (1991). 'Adjustment with a human face: a UNICEF record and perspective on the 1980s', *World Development*, 19(12), pp. 1807–1821.

Jolly, R. and Santos, R. (2016). 'From development of the "other" to global governance for universal and sustainable development', *IDS Bulletin*, 47(2), pp. 13–32.

Kabeer, N. (1994). *Reversed realities: gender hierarchies in development thought*. London: Verso.

Kabeer, N. (2012). *Women's economic empowerment and inclusive growth: labour markets and enterprise development*. London: Department for International Development.

Kallis, G. (2011). 'In defence of degrowth', *Ecological Economics*, 70(5), pp. 873–880.

Kallis, G. (2015). 'Degrowth', in Kallis, G., Demaria, F. and Alisa, G.D. (eds.) *Degrowth: a vocabulary for a new era*. London: Routledge, pp. 1–18.

Kallis, G., Kerschner, C. and Martinez-Alier, J. (2012). 'The economics of degrowth', *Ecological Economics*, 84, pp. 172–180.

Kallis, G., Kostakis, V., Lange, S., Muraca, B., Paulson, S. and Schmelzer, M. (2018). 'Research on degrowth', *Annual Review of Environment and Resources*, 43, pp. 291–316.

Kanbur, R. and Sumner, A. (2012). 'Poor countries or poor people? Development assistance and the new geography of global poverty', *Journal of International Development*, 24(6), pp. 686–695.

Kane, S.C. (2012). *Where rivers meet the sea: the political ecology of water*. Philadelphia: Temple University Press.

Kapoor, I. (2008). *The postcolonial politics of development*. London: Routledge.

Kapur, R. (2002). 'The tragedy of victimisation rhetoric: resurrecting the "native" subject in international/post-colonial feminist legal politics', *Harvard Human Rights Journal*, 15(1), pp. 1–38.

Katz, I. (2022). 'Mobile colonial architecture: facilitating settler colonialism's expansions, expulsions, resistance, and decolonisation', *Mobilities*, 17(2), pp. 213–237.

Keim, W. (2008). 'Social sciences internationally: the problem of marginalisation and its consequences for the discipline of sociology', *African Sociological Review*, 12(2), pp. 22–48.

Keynes, J. (1944). *Closing plenary session speech*. 22 July, Bretton Woods Conference.

Keynes, J.M. (1973). *The general theory of employment, interest and money*. London: Macmillan.

King, R. (1995). 'Migrations, globalisation and place', in Massey, D. and Jess, P. (eds.) *A place in the world*. Oxford: Oxford University Press, pp. 5–44

Kipling, R. (1899). *The white man's burden*. Available at: https://www.kiplingsociety.co.uk/poem/poems_burden.htm (accessed: 28 October 2022).

Klein, E. (2023). 'Towards a reparative welfare state', *New Political Economy*, 28(1), pp. 126–141.

Klein, E. and Morreo, C.E. (2019). *Postdevelopment in practice: alternatives, economies, ontologies*. London: Routledge.

Kothari, A., Salleh, A., Escobar, A., Demaria, F. and Acosta, A. (eds.) (2019). *Pluriverse: a post-development dictionary*. New York: Columbia University Press.

Kothari, U. (1997). 'Development discourse and post-colonial theory', *Asia-Pacific Journal of Rural Development*, 7(1), pp. 1–10.

Kothari, U. (2003). 'Staying put and staying poor?', *Journal of International Development: The Journal of the Development Studies Association*, 15(5), pp. 645–657.

Kothari, U. (2005). *A radical history of development studies: individuals, institutions and ideologies*. London: Zed Books.

Kothari, U. (2006a). 'Critiquing "race" and racism in development discourse and practice', *Progress in Development Studies*, 6(1), pp. 1–7.

Kothari, U. (2006b). 'An agenda for thinking about "race" in development', *Progress in Development Studies*, 6(1), pp. 9–23.

Kothari, U. (2007). 'Geographies and histories of development', *Journal für Entwicklungspolitik*, 23(2), pp. 28–44.

Kothari, U. (2008). 'Global peddlers and local networks: migrant cosmopolitanisms', *Environment and Planning D: Society and Space*, 26(3), pp. 500–516.

Kothari, U. (2009). 'The forced movement of colonised peoples and its impact on development', *Journal für Entwicklungspolitik*, 25(4), pp. 63–66.

Kothari, U. and Arnall, A. (2019). 'Everyday life and environmental change', *The Geographical Journal*, 185(2), pp. 130–141.

Kothari, U. and Minogue, M. (eds.) (2001). *Development theory and practice: critical perspectives*. New York: Red Globe.

Krueger, A.O. (1974). 'The political economy of the rent-seeking society', *American Economic Review*, 64(3), pp. 291–303.

Lal, D. (1985). *The poverty of development economics*. Cambridge, MA: MIT Press.

Lal, R., Hansen, D.O. and Uphoff, N. (eds.) (2002). *Food security and environmental quality in the developing world*. Boca Raton, FL: CRC Press.

Lambert, D. (2010). 'Black-Atlantic counterfactualism: speculating about slavery and its aftermath', *Journal of Historical Geography*, 36(3), pp. 286–296.

Lang, M. (2019). 'Plurinationality as a strategy: transforming local state institutions toward *Buen Vivir*', in Klein, E. and Morreo, C.D. (eds.) *Postdevelopment in practice: alternatives, economies, ontologies*. London: Routledge, pp. 176–189.

Larson, D.W. (2018). 'New perspectives on rising powers and global governance: status and clubs', *International Studies Review*, 20(2), pp. 247–254.

Le, M.H. (2020). 'Where be the "magic bullet" for educational change? Vietnam and the quest of policy borrowing from abroad', *Journal of Educational Change*, 21, pp. 455–466.

Lester, A. (2002). 'Obtaining the "due observance of justice": the geographies of colonial humanitarianism', *Environment and Planning D: Society and Space*, 20, pp. 277–293.

Lester, A. (2012). 'Humanism race and the colonial frontier', *Transactions of the Institute of British Geographers*, 37(1), pp. 132–148.

Lewis, D. (2019). '"Big D" and "little d": two types of twenty-first century development?' *Third World Quarterly*, 40(11), pp. 1957–1975.

Li, T.M. (2007). *The will to improve: governmentality, development, and the practice of politics*. Durham, NC: Duke University Press.

Li, T.M. (2010) 'To make live or let die? Rural dispossession and the protection of surplus populations', *Antipode*, 41, pp. 66–93.

Li, T.M. (2011). 'Rendering society technical: government through community and the ethnographic turn at the World Bank in Indonesia', in Mosse, D. (ed.) *Adventures in aidland: the anthropology of professionals in international development*. Oxford: Berghahn, pp. 57–80.

Li, X., Gu, J. and Zhang, C. (eds.) (2021). 'China and international development: knowledge, governance, and practice', *IDS Bulletin*, 52.2. https://

www.ids.ac.uk/publications/china-and-international-development-knowledge
-governance-and-practice/

Little, I. (1982). *Economic development: theories, practices, and international relations*. New York: Basic Books.

Loeser, J., Özler, B. and Premand, P. (2021). 'What have we learned about cash transfers?', *World Bank Blogs*, 10 May. Available at: https://blogs.worldbank.org/impactevaluations/what-have-we-learned-about-cash-transfers (accessed: 24 September 2022).

Loftus, A. (2019). 'Political ecology I: where is political ecology?', *Progress in Human Geography*, 43(1), pp. 172–183.

Lorde, A. (1983). 'The master's tools will never dismantle the master's house', in Moraga, C. and Alzandu'a, G. (eds.) *This bridge called my back*. New York: Kitchen Table Press, pp. 94–101.

Lyons, M. (2002). 'World conference against racism: new avenues for slavery reparations?', *Vanderbilt Journal of Transnational Law*, 35, pp. 1235–1265.

Mabogunje, A.L. (1989). 'Agrarian responses to outmigration in sub-Saharan Africa', *Population and Development Review*, 15, pp. 324–342.

Macfarlane, S.B., Jacobs, M. and Kaaya, E.E. (2008). 'In the name of global health: trends in academic institutions', *Journal of Public Health Policy*, 29, pp. 383–401.

Maldonado-Torres, N. (2007). 'On the coloniality of being: contributions to the development of a concept', *Cultural Studies*, 21(2–3), pp. 240–270.

Maldonado-Villalpando, E., Paneque-Galvez, J., Demaria, F. and Napoletano, B.M. (2022). 'Grassroots innovation for the pluriverse: evidence from Zapatismo and autonomous Zapatista education', *Sustainability Science*, 17, pp. 1301–1316.

Malone, B. (2015). 'Why Al Jazeera will not say Mediterranean "migrants"', *Al Jazeera*, 20 August. Available at: https://www.aljazeera.com/features/2015/8/20/why-al-jazeera-will-not-say-mediterranean-migrants (accessed: 10 June 2022).

Malthus, T. (1798). *An essay on the principle of population*. London: J. Johnson.

Mamdani, M. (1996). *Citizen and subject: contemporary Africa and the legacy of late colonialism*. London: James Currey.

Mamdani, M. (2020). *Neither settler nor native: making and unmaking of permanent minorities*. Cambridge, MA: Harvard University Press.

Mandel, E. (1991). 'The roots of the present crisis in the Soviet economy', *Socialist Register*, 27, pp. 194–210.

Mani, L. (1989). *Contentious traditions: the debate on sati in colonial India*. Berkeley: University of California Press.

Mann, J.M. (1997). 'Medicine and public health, ethics and human rights', *The Hastings Center Report*, 27(3), pp. 6–13.

Marchand, M. and Parpart, J.L. (eds.) (1995). *Feminism, postmodernism and development*. London: Routledge.

Massey, D. (1991). 'The political place of locality studies', *Environment and Planning A*, 23(2), pp. 267–281.

Massey, D. 1993. Power-geometry and a progressive sense of place, in Bird, J., Curtis, B., Putnam, T. and Tickner, L. (eds). *Mapping the futures: local culture, global change*. Routledge: London, pp. 75–85.

Massey, D. (2002). Entanglements of power: reflections, in Paddison, R., Philo, C., Routledge, P. and Sharp, J. (eds.) *Entanglements of power: geographies of domination/resistance*. London: Routledge, pp. 279–286.

Mawdsley, E. (2017). 'Development geography 1: cooperation, competition and convergence between "North" and "South"', *Progress in Human Geography*, 41(1), pp. 108–117.

Mawdsley, E. (2018). 'The "southernisation" of development?', *Asia Pacific Viewpoint*, 59(2), pp. 173–185.

Mawdsley, E. (2019). 'South–South cooperation 3.0? Managing the consequences of success in the decade ahead', *Oxford Development Studies*, 47(3), pp. 259–274.

Mawdsley, E. (2020). 'Queering development? The unsettling geographies of South–South cooperation', *Antipode*, 52(1), pp. 227–245.

Mawdsley, E. and Taggart, J. (2022). 'Rethinking d/Development', *Progress in Human Geography*, 46(1), pp. 3–20.

May, V.M. (2015). *Pursuing intersectionality, unsettling dominant imaginaries*. London: Routledge.

Mbembe, A. (2019). *Necropolitics*. Durham, NC: Duke University Press.

McArthur, J.W. and Rasmussen, K. (2017). 'How successful were the Millennium Development Goals?', *Brookings Blog*, 11 January. Available at: https://www.brookings.edu/blog/future-development/2017/01/11/how-successful-were-the-millennium-development-goals/ (accessed: 20 October 2022).

McAuliffe, P. (2021). 'Complicity or decolonization? Restitution of heritage from "global" ethnographic museums', *International Journal of Transitional Justice*, 15(3), pp. 678–689.

McClintock, A. (1994). 'The angel of progress: pitfalls of the term "postcolonialism"', in Barker, F., Hulme, P. and Iversen, M. (eds.) *Colonial discourse and postcolonial theory*. Manchester: Manchester University Press, pp. 291–304.

McClintock, A. (1995). *Imperial leather*. London: Routledge.

McConnell, F. and Woon, C.Y. (2021). 'Mapping Chinese diplomacy: relational contradictions and spatial tensions', *Geopolitics*. https://doi.org/10.1080/14650045.2021.1966417.

McEwan, C. (2001). 'Postcolonialism, feminism and development: intersections and dilemmas', *Progress in Development Studies*, 1(2), pp. 93–111.

McEwan, C. (2018). *Postcolonialism, decoloniality and development*. London: Routledge.

McLeod, J. (2020). 'Postcolonialism and feminism', in *Beginning postcolonialism*. 2nd edn. Manchester: Manchester University Press, pp. 197–233.

Mead, D.C. and Morrisson, C. (2004). 'The informal sector elephant', *World Development*, 24(10), pp. 1611–1619.

Meadows, D.H., Meadows, D.L., Randers, J. and Behrens III, W.W. (1972). *The limits to growth: a report for the Club of Rome's project on the predicament of mankind*. New York: Universe Books.

Mehmet, O. (1995). *Westernising the Third World*. London: Routledge.

Melber, H. (2019). 'Knowledge production, ownership and the power of definition: perspectives on and from sub-Saharan Africa', in Baud, I., Basile, E., Kontinen, T. and von Itter, S. (eds.) *Building development studies for the new millennium*. London: Palgrave Macmillan, pp. 265–287.

Mezzadra, S. and Stierl, M. (2020). 'What happens to freedom of movement during a pandemic?', *Open Democracy*, 24 March. Available at: https://www.opendemocracy.net/en/can-europe-make-it/what-happens-freedom-movement-during-pandemic/ (accessed: 22 October 2022).

Michalopoulos, S. and Papaioannou, E. (2016). 'The long-run effects of the scramble for Africa', *American Economic Review*, 106(7), pp. 1802–1848.

Miege, J.-L. (1980). 'The colonial past in the present', in Fischer, G. and Morris-Jones, W.H. (eds.) *Decolonisation and after: the British and French experience*. London: Routledge, pp. 35–49.

Mignolo, W.D. (2011). *The darker side of Western modernity: global futures, decolonial options*. Durham, NC: Duke University Press.

Mignolo, W.D. (2018). 'On pluriversality and multipolar world order: decoloniality after decolonization; de-Westernization after the Cold War', in Reiter, B. (ed.) *Constructing the pluriverse*. Durham, NC: Duke University Press, pp. 90–116.

Mignolo, W.D. (2020). 'On decoloniality: second thoughts', *Postcolonial Studies*, 23(4), pp. 612–618.

Mignolo, W.D. (2021). 'Coloniality and globalization: a decolonial take', *Globalizations*, 18(5), pp. 720–737.

Mignolo, W.D. and Walsh, C.E. (2018). *On decoloniality: concepts, analytics, praxis*. Durham, NC: Duke University Press.

Milanovic, B. (2016). *Global inequality: a new approach for the age of globalization*. Cambridge, MA: Harvard University Press.

Mills, C. (2007). 'The domination contract', in Pateman, C. and Mills, C. (eds.) *Contract and domination*. Cambridge: Polity Press, pp. 79–105.

Minh-Ha, T.T. (1987). 'Difference: a special Third World women issue', *Feminist Review*, 25, pp. 5–22.

Minh-Ha, T.T. (1989). *Woman, native, other: writing postcoloniality and feminism*. Bloomington: Indiana University Press.

Mitchell, W.J.T. (1987). *Iconology: image, text, ideology*. Chicago: University of Chicago Press.

Mohan, G. (2021). 'Below the belt? Territory and development in China's international rise', *Development and Change*, 52(1), pp. 54–75.

Mohanty, C.T. (1984). 'Under Western eyes: feminist scholarship and colonial discourses', *Boundary 2*, 12/13, pp. 333–358.

Mohanty, C.T. (1991). 'Under Western eyes: feminist scholarship and colonial discourses', in Mohanty, C.T., Russo, A. and Torres, L. (eds.) *Third World women and the politics of feminism*. Bloomington: Indiana University Press, pp. 196–220.

Mohanty, C.T. (1992). 'Feminist encounters: locating the politics of experience', in Barrett, M. and Phillips, A. (eds.) *Destabilising theory: contemporary feminist debates*. Cambridge: Polity Press, pp. 68–86.

Mohanty, C.T. (2003). '"Under Western eyes" revisited: feminist solidarity through anticapitalist struggles', *Signs: Journal of Women in culture and Society*, 28(2), pp. 499–535.

Mongia, P. (ed.) (1996). *Contemporary postcolonial theory*. London: Routledge.

Moore, J.W. (2017). 'The capitalocene, part I: on the nature and origins of our ecological crisis', *Journal of Peasant Studies*, 44(3), pp. 594–630.

Moore, S.A. (2008). 'The politics of garbage in Oaxaca, Mexico', *Society and Natural Resources*, 21(7), pp. 597–610.

Moore-Gilbert, B. (1997). *Postcolonial theory: contexts, practices, politics*. London: Verso.

Mora, C. and Piper, N. (eds.) (2021). *The Palgrave handbook of gender and migration*. London: Palgrave Macmillan.

Moseley, W., Carney, J. and Becker, B. (2010). 'Neoliberal policy, rural livelihoods, and urban food security in West Africa: a comparative study of The Gambia, Cote D'Ivoire and Mali', *PNAS*, 107(13), pp. 5774–5779.

Mosoetsa, S., Stillerman, J. and Tilly, C. (2016). 'Precarious labor, South and North: an introduction', *International Labor and Working-Class History*, 89, pp. 5–19.

Mosse, D. (2004). 'Is good policy unimplementable? Reflections on the "ethnography of aid policy and practice"', *Development and Change*, 35(4), pp. 639–671.

Mosse, D. (2005). 'Global governance and the ethnography of international aid', in Mosse, D. and Lewis, D. (eds.) *The aid effect: giving and governing in international development*. London: Pluto Press, pp. 1–36.

Mpofu, B. and Ndlovu-Gatsheni, S.J. (eds.) (2019). *Rethinking and unthinking development: perspectives on inequality and poverty in South Africa and Zimbabwe*. New York: Berghahn.

Muir, C., Rose, D. and Sullivan, P. (2010). 'From the other side of the knowledge frontier: Indigenous knowledge, social-ecological relationships and new perspectives'. *The Rangeland Journal*, 32(3), pp. 259–265.

Müller, M. (2020). 'In search of the global East: thinking between North and South', *Geopolitics*, 25(3), pp. 734–755.

Munck, R. (2013). 'The precariat: a view from the South', *Third World Quarterly*, 34(5), pp. 747–762.

Munck, R. and O'Hearn, D. (1999). *Critical development theory: contributions to a new paradigm*. London: Zed Books.

Nadvi, K. (2014). '"Rising powers" and labour and environmental standards', *Oxford Development Studies*, 42(2), pp. 137–150.

Naess, L.O. (2013). 'The role of local knowledge in adaptation to climate change', *WIREs Climate Change*, 4(2), pp. 99–106.

Navarro, V. (2002). *The political economy of social inequalities: consequences for health and quality of life*. Amityville, NY: Baywood Publishing Company.

Nielsen, L. (2011). *How to classify countries based on their level of development: how it is done and how it could be done*. International Monetary Fund Working Paper 11/31. Washington, DC: IMF.

Nkrumah, K. (1965). *Neo-colonialism, the last stage of imperialism*. New York: Penguin Classics.

North, M. (1883). *A vision of Eden*. London: Kew.

Noxolo, P. (2017). 'Decolonial theory in a time of the re-colonisation of UK research', *Transactions of the Institute of British Geographers*, 42(3), pp. 342–344.

Nussbaum, M.C. (2006). 'Education and democratic citizenship: capabilities and quality education', *Journal of Human Development*, 7(3), pp. 385–395.

Nyberg-Sørensen, N., Van Hear, N. and Engberg-Pedersen, P. (2002). 'The migration–development nexus: evidence and policy options. State-of-the-art overview', *International Migration*, 40(5), pp. 3–47.

Nyerere, J. (1977). 'The plea of the poor: new economic order needed for the world community', *New Directions*, 5(1), pp. 1–6.

Oakley, P. (1991). *Projects with people: the practice of participation in rural development*. Geneva: International Labour Office.

Okri, B. (2015) *A way of being free*. London: Head of Zeus.

Olivier de Sardan, J.P. (2008). *Anthropology and development: understanding contemporary social change*. London: Bloomsbury Publishing.

Oltermann, P. (2022). 'Germany hands over two Benin bronzes to Nigeria', *The Guardian*, 1 July. Available at: https://www.theguardian.com/world/ 2022/jul/01/germany-hands-over-two-benin-bronzes-to-nigeria (accessed: 19 September 2022).

O'Malley, A. and Clow, M. (2011). 'Political ecology: environmentalism for a change', in Henry, V. (ed.) *The critical development studies handbook: tools for change*. Halifax: Fernwood Publishing, pp. 214–218.

Organisation for Economic Co-operation and Development (OECD). (2015). *Multilateral aid 2015: Better partnerships for a post-2015 world*, Paris: OECD Publishing. https://doi.org/10.1787/9789264235212-en.

Oslender, U. (2019). 'Geographies of the pluriverse: decolonial thinking and ontological conflict on Colombia's Pacific coast', *Annals of the American Association of Geographers*, 109(6), pp. 1691–1705.

Parnwell, M. (1993). *Population movements and the Third World*. London: Routledge.

Parpart, J. (1995). 'Post-modernism, gender and development', in Crush, J. (ed.) *Power of development*. London: Routledge, pp. 253–265.

Patel, K. (2020). 'Race and a decolonial turn in development studies', *Third World Quarterly*, 41(9), pp. 1463–1475.

Patel, K. and North, A. (2022). 'An introduction to revisiting development studies education and an invitation to rethink teaching, learning and knowledge production in the neoliberal university', *Progress in Development Studies*, 22(3), pp. 211–221.

Patel, R. (2013). 'The long green revolution', *Journal of Peasant Studies*, 40(1), pp. 1–63.

Pearson, R. (2005). 'The rise of gender and development', in Kothari, U. (ed.) *A radical history of development studies: individuals, institutions and ideologies*. London: Zed Books, pp. 157–179.

Peet, R. and Watts, M. (1996). *Liberation ecologies: environment, development, social movements*. London: Routledge.

Peppiatt, D., Mitchell, J. and Holzmann, P. (2001). 'Cash transfers in emergencies: evaluating benefits and assessing risks', *Humanitarian Practice Network*, 35, pp. 1–28.

Pérez, M.S. and Saavedra, C.M. (2017). 'A call for onto-epistemological diversity in early childhood education and care: centering Global South conceptualizations of childhood/s', *Review of Research in Education*, 41(1), pp. 1–29.

Perry, K.K. (2021). 'The new "bond-age", climate crisis and the case for climate reparations: unpicking old/new colonialities of finance for development within the SDG', *Geoforum*, 126, pp. 361–371.

Phillips, R. (1996). *Mapping men and empire*. London: Routledge.

Pieterse, J.N. and Parekh, B. (eds.) (1995). *The decolonisation of imagination: culture, knowledge and power*. London: Zed Books.

Piketty, T. (2017). *Capital in the 21st century*. Cambridge, MA: Harvard University Press.

Piper, N. (2005). *Gender and migration. Policy analysis and research programme of the global commission on international migration*. Geneva: Global Commission on International Migration. Available at: https://www.incedes.org.gt/Master/pipersesentacuatro.pdf (accessed: 1 November 2021).

Power, M., Newell, P., Baker, L., Bulkeley, H., Kirshner, J. and Smith, A. (2016). 'The political economy of energy transitions in Mozambique and South Africa: the role of the rising power', *Energy Research & Social Science*, 17, pp. 10–19.

Prebisch, R. (1962). 'The economic development of Latin America and its principal problems', *Economic Bulletin for Latin America*, 7(1), pp. 1–51.

Preston, P. (1996). *Development theory: an introduction to the analysis of complex change*. Hoboken, NJ: Wiley-Blackwell.

Quijano, A. (2000). 'Coloniality of power, eurocentrism, and Latin America', *Nepantla: Views from South*, 1(3), pp. 533–580.

Quijano, A. (2007). 'Coloniality and modernity/rationality', *Cultural Studies*, 21(2–3), pp. 168–178.

Radcliffe, S. (1994). '(Representing) post-colonial women: authority, difference and feminisms', *Area*, 26(1), pp. 25–32.

Radcliffe, S. (2005). 'Development and geography: towards a postcolonial development geography?', *Progress in Human Geography*, 29(3), pp. 291–298.

Raghuram, P. (2009). 'Which migration, what development? Unsettling the edifice of migration and development', *Population, Space and Place*, 15(2), pp. 103–117.

Raghuram, P. and Madge, C. (2006). 'Towards a method for postcolonial development geography? Possibilities and challenges', *Singapore Journal of Tropical Geography*, 27(3), pp. 270–288.

Raghuram, P., Madge, C. and Noxolo, P. (2009). 'Rethinking responsibility and care for a postcolonial world', *Geoforum*, 40(1), pp. 5–13.

Raghuram, P., Noxolo, P. and Madge, C. (2014). 'Rising Asia and postcolonial geography', *Singapore Journal of Tropical Geography*, 35(1), pp. 119–135.

Rahnema, M. and Bawtree, V. (eds.) (1997). *The post-development reader*. London: Zed Books.

Rambukwella, H. (2022). 'Patriotic science: the COVID-19 pandemic and the politics of indigeneity and decoloniality in Sri Lanka', *Interventions*, 1–18. https://doi.org/10.1080/1369801X.2022.2158488.

Ravallion, M. (2009). 'Do poorer countries have less capacity for redistribution?', *Journal of Globalization and Development*, 1(2). https://doi.org/10.2202/1948-1837.1105.

Ravallion, M. (2012). 'Should we care equally about poor people wherever they may live?', *World Bank Blogs*, 8 November. Available at: https://blogs.

worldbank.org/developmenttalk/should-we-care-equally-about-poor-people-wherever-they-may-live (accessed: 10 June 2022).

Ravallion, M. (2014). 'Income inequality in the developing world', *Science*, 344(6186), pp. 851–855.

Reiter, B. (2018). *Constructing the pluriverse: the geopolitics of knowledge*. Durham, NC: Duke University Press.

Reuveny, R.X. and Thompson, W.R. (2007). 'The North–South divide and international studies: a symposium', *International Studies Review*, 9(4), pp. 556–564.

Reynolds, H. (1996). *Aboriginal sovereignty: reflections on race, state & nation*. Crow's Nest, Sydney: Allen & Unwin.

Ricardo, D. (1912). *The principles of political economy and taxation*. London: J.M. Dent & Sons.

Richey, L.A. and Ponte, S. (2011). *Brand aid: shopping well to save the world*. Minneapolis: University of Minnesota Press.

Rickards, L.A. (2015). 'Metaphor and the Anthropocene: presenting humans as a geological force', *Geographical Research*, 53(3), pp. 280–287.

Rist, G. (1997). *The history of development: from Western origins to global faith*. London: Zed Books.

Rizzo, M. (2011). '"Life is war": informal transport workers and neoliberalism in Tanzania 1998–2009', *Development and Change*, 42(5), pp. 1179–1206.

Robbins, P. (2019). *Political ecology: a critical introduction*. 3rd edn. Hoboken, NJ: Wiley Blackwell.

Robinson, C.J. (2000). *Black Marxism: the making of the Black radical tradition*. Chapel Hill: University of North Carolina Press.

Rodney, W. (1972). *How Europe underdeveloped Africa*. London: Bogle-L'Ouverture.

Rostow, W.W. (1990). *The stages of economic growth: a non-communist manifesto*. 3rd edn. Cambridge: Cambridge University Press.

Ruz, C. (2015). 'The battle over the word used to describe immigrants', *BBC News*, 28 August. Available at: https://www.bbc.com/news/magazine-34061097 (accessed: 10 July 2022).

Sachs, J.D. (2006). *The end of poverty: economic possibilities for our time*. London: Penguin Books.

Sachs, W. (ed.) (1992). *Development dictionary: a guide to knowledge as power*. London: Zed Books.

Sachs, W. (ed.) (2010). *The development dictionary: a guide to knowledge as power*. 2nd ed. London: Zed Books.

Said, E. (1979). *Orientalism*. New York: Vintage.

Said, E. (1981). *Covering Islam: how the media and the experts determine how we see the rest of the world*. New York: Vintage.

Said, E. (1989). 'Representing the colonised: anthropology's interlocutors', *Critical Inquiry*, 15(2), pp. 205–225.

Sassen, S. (1996). *Losing control? Sovereignty in an age of globalization*. New York: Columbia University Press.

Sassen, S. (2014). *Expulsions: brutality and complexity in the global economy*. Cambridge, MA: Harvard University Press.

Saunders, P. (2017). *Welfare to work in practice: social security and participation in economic and social life*. London: Routledge.

Schalk, O. (2022). 'Human rights tribunal rules Indigenous compensation plan insufficient', *Canadian Dimension*, 26 October. Available at: https://canadiandimension.com/articles/view/human-rights-tribunal-rules-indigenous-compensation-plan-insufficient (accessed: 20 November 2022).

Schirch, L. (2022). *Decolonising peacebuilding: a way forward out of crisis.* Berlin: Berghof Foundation.

Self Employed Women's Association. (2014). *A little more, how much it is … Piloting basic income transfers in Madhya Pradesh, India.* Available at: https://sewabharat.org/wp-content/uploads/2021/09/Executive-Summary.pdf.

Sen, A. (1988). *The standard of living.* Cambridge: Cambridge University Press.

Sen, A. (1999). *Development as freedom.* Oxford: Oxford University Press.

Sen, A. (2009). *The idea of justice.* London: Penguin.

Sheller, M. (2003). *Consuming the Caribbean: from Arawaks to zombies.* London: Routledge.

Sheller, M. (2018). *Mobility justice: the politics of movement in an age of extremes.* London: Verso.

Sheller, M. (2021). *Advanced introduction to mobilities.* Cheltenham, UK, and Northampton, MA: Edward Elgar Publications.

Sheller, M. and Urry, J. (2006). 'The new mobilities paradigm', *Environment and Planning A: Economy and Space*, 38(2), pp. 207–226.

Shilliam, R. (2014). 'Race and development', in Weber, H. (ed.) *Politics of development.* London: Routledge, pp. 31–48.

Shohat, E. (1992). 'Notes on the "post-colonial"', *Social Text*, 31/32, pp. 99–113.

Shohat, E. and Stam R. (1994). *Unthinking eurocentrism: multiculturalism and the media.* London: Routledge.

Sidaway, J.D. (2012). 'Geographies of development: new maps, new visions?', *The Professional Geographer*, 64(1), pp. 49–62.

Sikor, T. (2013). *The justices and injustices of ecosystem services.* London: Routledge.

Silova, I., Millei, Z. and Piattoeva, N. (2017). 'Interrupting the coloniality of knowledge production in comparative education: postsocialist and postcolonial dialogues after the Cold War', *Comparative Education Review*, 61(S1), pp. S74–S102.

Silverstone R. (2006). *Media and morality: on the rise of the mediapolis.* Cambridge: Polity Press.

Silvey, R. and Rankin, K. (2011). 'Development geography: critical development studies and political geographic imaginaries', *Progress in Human Geography*, 35(5), pp. 696–704.

Smith, A. (1776). *An inquiry into the nature and causes of the wealth of nations.* London: W. Strahan and T. Cadell.

Smith, L.T. (1999). *Decolonizing methodologies: research and Indigenous peoples.* London: Zed Books.

Solarz, M.W. (2017). 'The birth and development of the language of global development in light of trends in global population, international politics, economics and globalisation', *Third World Quarterly*, 38(8), pp. 1753–1766.

Spivak, G.C. (1988). 'Can the subaltern speak?', in Nelson, C. and Grossberg, L. (eds.) *Marxism and the interpretation of culture.* London: Macmillan Education, pp. 271–313.

Spivak, G.C. (1993). *Outside the teaching machine*. London: Routledge.

Standing, G. (2014). *A precariat charter: from denizens to citizens*. London: Bloomsbury Academic.

Standing, G. (2015). 'Why basic income's emancipatory value exceeds its monetary value', *Basic Income Studies*, 10(2), pp. 193–223.

Standing, H. and Taylor, P. (2016). 'Whose knowledge counts? Development studies institutions and power relations in a globalised world', *IDS Bulletin*, 47(6), pp. 169–178.

Stanley, H.M. (1889). *Through the dark continent, or the sources of the Nile around the great lakes of Equatorial Africa and down the Livingstone River to the Atlantic Ocean*. London: Sampson Low, Marston, Searle & Rivington.

Stjernø, S. (2005). *Solidarity in Europe: the history of an idea*. Cambridge: Cambridge University Press.

Streeten, P. (1999). *Ten years of human development: special contribution*. Oxford: Oxford University Press.

Sultana, F. (2021). 'Political ecology 1: From margins to center', *Progress in Human Geography*, 45(1), pp. 156–165.

Sylvester, C. (2006). 'Bare life as a development/postcolonial problematic', *Geographical Journal*, 172(1), pp. 66–77.

Táíwò, O.O. (2022). *Reconsidering reparations*. Oxford: Oxford University Press.

Tănăsescu, M. (2017). 'When a river is a person: from Ecuador to New Zealand, nature gets its day in court', *Open rivers: Rethinking water, place and community*, June 2017. Available at: https://openrivers.lib.umn.edu/article/when-a-river -is-a-person-from-ecuador-to-new-zealand-nature-gets-its-day-in-court/#:~: text=Things%20are%20going%20better%20in,law%3B%20it%20has%20legal %20standing (accessed: 16 August 2022).

Tanner, T. and Allouche, J. (2011). 'Towards a new political economy of climate change and development', *IDS Bulletin*, 42(3), pp. 1–14.

Tarantola, D., Gruskin, S., Brown, T.M. and Fee, E. (2006). 'Jonathan Mann: founder of the health and human rights movement', *American Journal of Public Health*, 96(11), pp. 1942–1943.

Tengö, M., Brondizio, E.S., Elmqvist, T., Malmer, P. and Spierenburg, M. (2014). 'Connecting diverse knowledge systems for enhanced ecosystem governance: the multiple evidence base approach', *Ambio*, 43(5), pp. 579–591.

Tengö, M., Hill, R., Malmer, P., Raymond, C.M., Spierenburg, M., Danielsen, F., Elmqvist, T. and Folke, C. (2017). 'Weaving knowledge systems in IPBES, CBD and beyond—lessons learned for sustainability', *Current Opinion in Environmental Sustainability*, 26, pp. 17–25.

Thobani, S. (2005). 'Review of the book *Feminism without Borders: Decolonizing Theory, Practicing Solidarity*', *Hypatia*, 20(3), pp. 221–224.

Tikly, L. (2009). 'Chapter 2: Education and the new imperialism', *Counterpoints*, 369, pp. 23–45. http://www.jstor.org/stable/42980379.

Todaro, M. and Smith, S. (2015). *Economic development*. 12th edn. Harlow: Pearson.

Toye, J. (1993). *Dilemmas of development: reflections on the counter-revolution in development theory and policy*. 2nd edn. Oxford: Blackwell.

Tronto, J. (2003). 'Time's place', *Feminist Theory*, 4(2), pp. 119–138.

Tuck, E. and Yang, W.K. (2012). 'Decolonization is not a metaphor', *Decolonization: Indigeneity, Education & Society*, 1(1), pp. 1–40.

Tynan, L. (2021). 'What is relationality? Indigenous knowledges, practices and responsibilities with kin', *Cultural Geographies*, 28(4), pp. 597–610.

Tyszczuk, R. (2016). 'Anthropocene unconformities: on the aporias of geological space and time', *Space and Culture*, 19(4), pp. 435–447.

Uitto, J. (ed.) (2021). *Evaluating environment in international development*. London: Routledge.

United Nations International Children's Emergency Fund (UNICEF). (1987). *Adjustment with a human face*. UNICEF.

UN Development Programme. (1990). *Human development report 1990: concept and measurement of human development*. New York: United Nations.

UN High Commissioner for Refugees. (2012). *An introduction to cash-based interventions in UNHCR operations*. Available at: http://www.unhcr.org/515a959e9 .pdf (accessed: 9 August 2017).

UN Women. (2006). *An in-depth study on all form of violence against women*. Available at: https://www.un.org/womenwatch/daw/vaw/SGstudyvaw.htm (accessed: 20 January 2017).

Uphoff, N. (1988). 'Assisted self-reliance: working with, rather than for the poor', in Lewis, J.P. (ed.) *Strengthening the poor: what have we learned?* Washington, DC: Transaction Books, pp. 47–59.

Van Parijs, P (2006). 'Basic income: a simple and powerful idea for the twenty-first century', in Ackermann, B., Alstott, A. and Van Parijs, P. (eds.) *Redesigning distribution: basic income and stakeholder grants as cornerstones for an egalitarian capitalism*. London: Verso, pp. 4–40.

Vanyoro, K.P. (2019). 'Decolonising migration research and potential pitfalls: reflections from South Africa', *Pambazuka News*, 17 May. Available at: https://www.academia.edu/39172651/Decolonising_migration_research_and _potential_pitfalls_Reflections_from_South_Africa (accessed: 12 May 2022).

Viveiros de Castro, E. (2013). 'The relative native', *HAU: Journal of Ethnographic Theory*, 3(3), pp. 473–502.

Wainwright, J. (2008). *Decolonizing development: colonial power and the Maya*. Oxford: Wiley Blackwell.

Walsh, C.E. (2020). 'Decolonial learnings, askings and musings', *Postcolonial Studies*, 23(4), pp. 604–611.

Ward, E. (2019). 'The tide of change: open letter from Esme Ward', *Museum-ID*. Available at: https://museum-id.com/the-tide-of-change-open-letter-from-esme-ward/ (accessed: 20 October 2022).

Waring, M. (1999). *Counting for nothing: what men value and what women are worth*. Toronto: Toronto University Press.

wa Thiong'o, N. (1986). *Decolonising the mind: the politics of language in African literature*. London: James Currey.

Weeks, K. (2011). *The problem with work: feminism, Marxism, antiwork politics, and postwork imaginaries*. Durham, NC: Duke University Press.

Weiner, M. (1990). *The child and the state in India: child labor and education policy in comparative perspective*. Princeton, NJ: Princeton University Press.

Weiqiang, L., Lindquist, J., Xiang, B. and Yeoh, B.S.A. (2017). 'Migration infrastructures and the production of migrant mobilities', *Mobilities*, 12(2), pp. 167–174.

Whitehead, C. (2005). 'The historiography of British imperial education policy, part I: India', *History of Education*, 34(3), pp. 315–329.

Williams, E. (1944). *Capitalism and slavery*. Chapel Hill: University of North Carolina Press.

Willis, K. and Yeoh, B. (2000). *Gender and migration*. Cheltenham, UK, and Northampton, MA: Edward Elgar Publishing.

Wilson, C. (2001). 'Decolonizing methodologies: research and Indigenous peoples', *Social Policy Journal of New Zealand*, 17, pp. 214–218.

Wilson, K. (2012). *Race, racism and development: interrogating history, discourse and practice*. London: Zed Books.

Woetzel, J., Madgavkar, A., Ellingrud, K., Labaye, E., Devillard, S., Kutcher, E., Manyika, J., Dobbs, R. and Krishnan, M. (2015). *How advancing women's equality can add $12 trillion to global growth*. Washington, DC: McKinsey & Company. Available at: http://www.mckinsey.com/global-themes/employment -and-growth/how-advancing-womens-equality-can-add-12-trillion-to-global-growth (accessed: 11 July 2016).

Wolfe, P. (2006). 'Settler colonialism and the elimination of the native', *Journal of Genocide Research*, 8(4), pp. 387–409.

Worboys, M. (1976). 'The emergence of tropical medicine: a study in the establishment of a scientific specialty', in Lemaine, G., Macleod, R., Mulkay, M. and Weingart, P. (eds.) *Perspectives on the emergence of scientific disciplines*. The Hague: Mount & Co., pp. 75–98.

World Bank. (1983). *World development report 1983*. Oxford: Oxford University Press.

World Bank. (2016). *Women, business and the law 2016*. Washington, DC: World Bank.

World Health Organization. (2018). *Millennium Development Goals (MDGs)*. Available at: https://www.who.int/news-room/fact-sheets/detail/millennium-development-goals-(mdgs) (accessed: 20 October 2022).

Yanacopulos, H. and Smith, M.B. (2007). 'The ambivalent cosmopolitanism of international NGOs', in Bebbington, A., Hickey, S. and Mitlin, D.C. (eds.) *Can NGOs make a difference? The challenge of development alternatives*. London: Zed, pp. 298–315.

Young, R. (1990). *White mythologies: writing history and the West*. London: Routledge.

Zanotti, L., Carothers, C., Apok, C.A., Huang, S., Coleman, J. and Ambrozek, C. (2020). 'Political ecology and decolonial research: co-production with the Iñupiat in Utqiaġvik', *Journal of Political Ecology*, 27(1), pp. 43–66.

Zarakol, A. (2019). '"Rise of the rest": as hype and reality', *International Relations*, 33(2), pp. 213–228.

Ziai, A. (2007). *Exploring post-development: theory and practice, problems and perspectives*. London: Routledge.

Ziai, A. (2017). *Development discourse and global history: from colonialism to the Sustainable Development Goals*. London: Routledge.

Index

Abrahamsen, R. 38
Abuja Proclamation 109
accumulation 43, 49–51, 60
Acemoglu, D. 31
actors 36–7
affective responses 39
Africa
        cash transfers 65
        'Dark Continent' 29
        partitioning of 31
agents 36–7
aid 8, 21, 32, 36
AIDS epidemic 70
Al-Jazeera 80–81
Alma-Ata Declaration 69
Anthias, F. 49
Anthropocene, the 91
Appadurai, A. 79
assimilation 16
Australia 29–30, 105
        'White Australian Policy' 30
Australian Institute of Aboriginal and
        Torres Strait Islander Studies
        (AIATSIS) 105

Baldwin, J. 30
Ban Ki-moon 103
Bandung Conference of 1955 40
basic income (BI) approach 66–7
Bastia, T. 86
BBC 80
Belt and Road Initiative (BRI) 5, 23, 40
Benhabib, S. 86
Benin bronzes 105
Berlin Conference of 1885 31
Bhabha, H. 45

'big D' Development 3–4, 35
Bill and Melinda Gates Foundation 70
binaries 7
        migration 78
        North–South 11, 21, 32–3, 33–4,
                35, 41
biodiversity loss 89
Black Lives Matter movement 1, 54
borders 27–42
        bordering practices and mobilities
                76–7
        challenging spatial borders
                and new geographies of
                development 33–5
        historical representations 28–31
        migration policies and open vs
                restricted 84
        rising powers and South–South
                cooperation 39–42
        spatial demarcations 31–3
'brain drain' 81–2
Brazil, India, China and South Africa
        (BICS) 39–42
Brazil, Russia, India, China and South
        Africa (BRICS) 5
Bretton Woods institutions 7, 13,
        20–21, 36
        see also under individual
                institutions
Brundtland Report 92
Buen Vivir 98–100, 113
Buffett, P. 37
Büscher, B. 35

campaigns 37–9, 102–3
Campbell, D. 38, 39

Canada 109
capabilities 24–6
capitalism 3–4, 35, 42, 90
    accumulation through
        dispossession and
        expulsion 43, 49–51, 60
    'cool' 103
    degrowth and dealing with 96–8
carbon dioxide emissions 88
Caribbean Community (CARICOM)
    110
caring work, unpaid 62–3
Carpio, G. 86–7
cash transfers (CTs) 64–5, 67
    unconditional cash transfers 65
Castree, N. 90
charity 36–7, 102–3
Chatterjee, P. 50
Cheeseman, N. 30
China 5, 23, 39–40
    Belt and Road Initiative (BRI) 5,
        23, 40
Chipko movement 96
Chouliaraki, L. 38, 103, 104
Christian missionaries, education by
    72
Chuji, M. 99
classifications 10, 27–42
    actors and agents 36–7
    historical representations 28–31
    migration 78
    Western public and popular
        representations of
        development 37–9
climate change 10, 33, 88–9, 94, 97
    reparations and climate justice
        110
    see also environmental
        degradation
Clow, M. 94
Collins, P.H. 48–9
colonialism 6–7, 13, 14, 15–17, 43–4,
    56, 58, 90
    categorisations 28–31
    education 72–3
    employment and labour 61
    and migration 86–7
    neo-colonialism 16, 18, 30–31

political ecology and 96
postcolonialism 43, 44–6, 58
reparations for 109–10
repatriation of colonial objects
    104–6
settler colonialism 15–17, 29–30,
    86–7
coloniality 16, 18–19
    degrowth and 98
    education 74
'Combahee River Collective
    Statement' 48
commodification 38
community economies approach 113
comparative advantage 19–20
compartmentalisation 7
conditional cash transfers (CCTs)
    64–5
conscientisation 75
constellations of mobility 85
consumption 103
convergence 33–5
Cooke, B. 17, 53
'cool capitalism' 103
corporations 36–7
Correa, R. 99
COVID-19 pandemic 1, 67, 71, 76, 100
Cowen, M. 3
Cresswell, T. 83, 85
critical ideas and approaches 10, 43–58
    accumulation through
        dispossession and
        expulsion 43, 49–51
    decolonisation and decoloniality
        43, 54–8
    feminisms and intersectionality
        43, 46–9, 57, 58
    Indigenous knowledges and
        ontologies 43, 52–4, 58
    postcolonialism 43, 44–6, 58
    post-development 43, 51–2, 58
Crush, J. 2, 39, 44
Cueto, M. 69
cultural sensitivity 57
culture and development 57
Currie-Alder, B. 8–9

D'Costa, A. 60

decolonial degrowth approach 98
decoloniality 6–7, 11, 43, 54–8, 101,
    106–8
    decolonisation of development
        54–8
    migration, development and 84–7
decommodification 66–7
definitions of development 2–4
degrowth 96–8
Delgado Wise, R. 82
Dengler, C. 98
dependency theories 21–2
development assistance/aid 8, 21, 32,
    36
Development Assistance Committee
    (DAC) 32
development histories and ideas,
    see mainstream development
    histories and ideas
development industry 36–7, 102,
    107–8
disease eradication programmes 68–9
displacement 60–61
dispossession 24, 43, 49–51, 60–61
division of labour 19
    gendered 62–4
donor countries 36
Douzinas, C. 90
Drissi, S. 91
Du Bois, W.E.B. 28

Earth Rights 98–100
economic growth 5, 7, 19–24, 26, 41–2
    classification by 31–2
    degrowth 96–8
    and environmental degradation
        92–4
economic migrants 77
Ecuador 98, 99
Edensor, T. 100
education 10, 59–60, 72–5
Elson, D. 62
employment 10, 59–67, 75
    cash transfers 64–5, 67
    decommodification of labour and
        work 66–7
    gendered work 62–4
    informal economy 61–2

Enlightenment 90
enslavement, reparations for 109–10
environmental degradation 10, 51,
    88–100
    development and 89–94
    and human/non-human
        distinctions 89–91
environmental sustainability 10,
    88–100
    Buen Vivir and Earth Rights
        98–100
    degrowth 96–8
    development and 89, 91–4
    political ecology 95–6
Escobar, A. 1, 11, 44, 51–2, 59, 111,
    112
Esson, J. 56, 57
Esteva, G. 51, 111
ethnoscapes 79
eugenics 30
Eurocentrism 6, 14, 44, 96
exhibition spaces 28–9
explorations 28–30
expulsion 49–51

Farmer, P. 67, 69
Fassin, D. 103
Featherstone, D. 102
feminisms 43, 46–9, 57, 58
feminist political ecology 96
Ferguson, J. 65
Fiddian-Qasmiyeh, E. 86
financescapes 79
financialisation 50, 51
Fiszbein, A. 64
flows, migration and 79–80
fossil fuels 94
Framework Convention on Climate
    Change 88
Frankel, B. 93
Fraser, N. 63
free market 19–20, 22–3
freedoms 24–6
Freire, P. 75
friction of distance 83
future orientation 8, 14

Galien, C. 106–7

Gandhian Economy of Permanence 98
Gender and Development (GAD)
    approaches 47, 57
gendered work 62–4
Germany 105, 109
Getachew, A. 22
Gibson, C. 94
Gibson-Graham, J.K. 113
Gills, B.K. 40, 112
Gini coefficient 26
global challenges and events 1, 33–5,
    101
global 'colour line' 28
global development 8, 34–5
Global Financial Crisis of 2008 23
global health 71–2
Global North 11, 21, 32–3
Global South 11, 18–19, 21, 32–3
    South–South cooperation 5, 23–4,
    39–42
Godlewska, A. 17
Goldsmith, E. 17
Goodyear-Ka'ōpua, N. 16
Gordon, J.A. 55
Gordon, L.R. 55
Gray, K. 40
'great convergence' 33–5
Great Depression 20
Green Revolution 93
grief 100
Griffiths, I. 31
Grosfoguel, R. 56, 74, 86
Gudynas, E. 99
Guijt, I. 53

Hage, G. 54, 90
Hammar, T. 81
Harding, S. 46
Hart, G. 3
Harvey, D. 50, 83
Head, L. 100
health 10, 59–60, 67–72, 75
    disease eradication programmes
    68–9
    global health 71–2
    primary health care 69–70
    right to 70–71
Hickel, J. 61, 97, 98

historical perspective 6–7
    borders and classifications 28–31
    migration 85–6
Holbraad, M. 53
Holocaust reparations 109
hookworm 68
hope 100
Horner, R. 34, 35
Hosseini, S.A.H. 112
Hulme, D. 34, 35
human development 19, 24–6
Human Development Index (HDI)
    25–6, 36
human/non-human distinctions
    89–91
humanitarianism 30
Hutchings, K. 111, 112

ideoscapes 79
Igwe, I.O.C. 21
imagery 38–9
immanent process 3
imperialism 14, 15–17, 18
inclusion 74–5
income level 32
independence, national 16
India 15, 60, 72–3
    Universal Basic Income (UBI)
    66–7
Indigenous
    knowledges 6, 43, 52–4, 58
    education and inclusion 74–5
    ontologies 52–4
Indigenous peoples
    decoloniality 55–6
    elimination 15–16
    and the environment 90, 91–2,
    95–6
    mobility 86–7
individualism 103
industrial revolution 90
inequality 26, 28, 33, 35
    migration and 82
informal economy 61–2
intentional practice 3
interconnectedness of places 79
Intergovernmental Panel on Climate
    Change (IPCC) 88–9

international aid industry 8
International Bank for
    Reconstruction and
    Development 20
International Labour Organization
    (ILO) 62
International Monetary Fund (IMF)
    20, 23, 36, 69–70
International Organization for
    Migration (IOM) 80
internment camps 109
intersectionality 43, 46–9

Jarosz, L. 29
Jolly, R. 24
justice 101, 102–6

Kallis, G. 96–7
Kapur, R. 48
Katz, I. 87
Kenyans, reparations to 109
Keynes, J.M. 20–21
Keynesianism 20–21, 22–3
Kothari, U. 53, 78–9, 112

labour
    division of, *see* division of labour
    employment and, *see*
        employment
land 15–16
    displacement and dispossession
        60–61
land grabs 51
landscape 29
Lang, M. 98–9
Latin America 16, 21, 68
    Buen Vivir 98–100, 113
Le, M.H. 73, 74
Lewis, D. 2–3
Li, T.M. 19
liberal feminism 46
linearity 111
'little d' development 3–4, 35
local knowledge 53
localism 52
Loftus, A. 96
Lorde, A. 55
Loss and Damage 110

Macaulay, T. 72–3
MacFarlane, S.B. 71
mainstream development histories
    and ideas 10, 13–26
    colonialism 13, 14, 15–17
    economic growth 19–24, 26
    human development 19, 24–6
    modernisation, coloniality and
        emergence of post-war
        development 18–19
Maldonado-Villalpando, E. 95–6
Malone, B. 81
Malthus, T. 92
Mamdani, M. 17
Manchester Museum 105
Manson, P. 67
Márquez Covarrubias, H. 82
Marshall Plan 21
Massey, D. 79, 104
Mau Mau rebellion 109
Mawdsley, E. 3–4, 5, 24, 33, 40, 41
May, V.M. 49
McAuliffe, P. 104–5
Meadows, D.H. 92
meanings of development 2–4
measurement of education levels 74
media 37–9
mediascapes 79
Mediterranean refugee crisis 80–81,
    103
Mehmet, O. 44
Michalopoulos, S. 31
migration 10, 76–87
    defining 78–81
    and development approaches
        81–4
    development, decoloniality and
        84–7
migration–development nexus 82–4
migration policies 83–4
Millennium Development Goals
    (MDGs) 13, 34, 71, 72, 73
missionary education 72
mobilities 10, 76–87
    defining 78–81
    development, decoloniality and
        84–7
    new mobilities paradigm 84–6

mobility sovereignty 86–7
modernisation 3, 4, 7, 18–19, 43
Mohan, G. 5
Mohanty, C.T. 48
Moore, J. 91
multipolarity 5–6
Munck, R. 61

Namibia 67
Nasser, G.A. 40
national independence 16
Nehru, J. 40
neo-colonialism 16, 18, 30–31
neoliberalism 22–3, 103
    health care policies 69–70
new geographies of development 33–5
New International Economic Order
    7, 22, 40
new mobilities paradigm 84–6
Nigeria 105
Nkrumah, K. 18
Non-Aligned Movement 40–41
noneconomic activities 113
nongovernmental organisations
    (NGOs) 33
non-human/human distinctions
    89–91
non-Western perspectives 6
norms
    gendered 63
    Western 59
North, M. 29
North/South distinction 11, 21, 32–3,
    33–4, 35, 41
Noxolo, P. 54, 56, 106, 107
Nussbaum, M. 25
Nyere, J.K. 22

Official Development Assistance
    (ODA) 32
Okri, B. 53
Oltermann, P. 105
O'Malley, A. 94
oppressed, pedagogy of the 75
Organisation of African Unity 109
Organisation for Economic
    Co-operation and Development
    (OECD) 32

Oslender, U. 111, 113

Pan-African Conference on
    Reparations for Enslavement
    and Colonisation 109
Papaioannou, E. 31
Parnwell, M. 78
participatory development 53, 57
Parzinger, H. 105
pedagogy of the oppressed 75
periodisation 7, 13–14
philanthropy 36–7, 70
pluriversality 6, 11, 52, 101, 111–13
political ecology 95–6
politics of interrelation 104
popular representations of
    development 37–9
population growth 92
postcolonial feminism 58
postcolonialism 35, 43, 44–6, 58
post-development 43, 51–2, 58
post-war development 18–19
post-war reconstruction 20–21
poverty 33
    migration and 82–3
primary health care 69–70
progress 43, 111
public–private partnerships 70

racism 30
Radcliffe, S. 35
Raghuram, P. 87, 108
Rankin, K. 4
redistribution 101, 104, 108–10
refugees 77, 80–81, 103
remittances 81, 82
Rengifo, G. 99
reparations 101, 108–10
repatriation of colonial objects 104–6
representations of development 37–9
residential schools 109
revolutionary development 35
'Rhodes Must Fall' campaign 54
Ricardo, D. 19–20
right to health 70–71
Rio Earth Summit 88
rising powers 5, 39–42
Robbins, P. 95

Robinson, C.J. 55
Rockefeller Foundation 68, 93
Rodney, W. 15
Ross, R. 67
Rostow, W.W. 21

Sachs, W. 43–4
Said, E. 16, 28–9, 54, 106
Sassen, S. 50–51, 84
'scapes' of global flows 79
Schady, N.R. 64
Seebacher, L.M. 98
Selective Primary Health Care Plan 69
Self Employed Women's Association
     (SEWA) 66
Sen, A. 25
settler anchoring 86–7
settler colonialism 15–17, 29–30, 86–7
sexual harassment 64
Shah, M. 53
Sheller, M. 76, 84–5, 86, 87
Shenton, R.W. 3
Sikor, T. 95
Silk Road 23
Silvey, R. 4
Singer–Prebisch thesis 20
Smith, A. 19, 20
Smith, N. 17
Smithsonian Institution 105
Social Darwinism 30
social spending 70
socio-economic change 3
Solarz, M.W. 11, 32
solidarity 11, 101, 102–6
South–South cooperation 5, 23–4,
     39–42
southernisation of development 5, 41
spatial demarcations 7–8, 31–3
     challenging 33–5
Standing, G. 60
Stanley, H. 29
structural adjustment programmes
     (SAPs) 23, 69–70
subsistence economies 61
Sukarno, President 40
Sultana, F. 96
sustainability, see environmental
     sustainability

Sustainable Development Goals
     (SDGs) 13, 34, 60, 71, 72, 74–5,
     89, 102
Sylvester, C. 45

Taggart, J. 3–4
Táíwò, O.O. 110
Tănăsescu, M. 99
technical assistance 59–60
technological innovation 18–19
     development and sustainability
          93–4
technoscapes 79
temporal demarcations 7, 8, 13–14
terra nullius 29–30
Third World Difference 48
Third World Quarterly 55
'Third World Woman' 48
Toye, J. 23
transnationalism 79–80
Tronto, J. 108
tropical medicine 67–8
Truman, H.S. 18–19
Tuck, E. 57, 107, 108
Tynan, L. 53

ubuntu 98, 113
Uitto, J. 100
underdevelopment 15, 21–2, 82
unemployment 51
UNESCO 'Education for All' 73
UNICEF 66, 70
United Kingdom (UK)
     colonial rule in Australia 29–30
     imperialism in India 15
     reparations to Kenyans 109
United Nations (UN) 7, 17, 36, 80
     Decade for Women 47
     Framework Convention on
          Climate Change 88
     Millennium Development Goals
          (MDGs) 13, 34, 71, 72,
          73
     Permanent Forum on
          Indigenous Issues 91
     Sustainable Development Goals
          (SDGs) 13, 34, 60, 71, 72,
          74–5, 89, 102

United Nations Development
Programme (UNDP) 24–5,
25–6
Human Development Index
25–6, 36
Human Development Report
25, 36
United Nations High Commissioner
for Refugees (UNHCR) 65
United States (US) 17, 20
Marshall Plan 21
reparations payments 109
technological innovation 18–19
universal capabilities 25
universalism 111, 112
Urry, J. 84–5

Vietnam 73, 74
violence against women and girls 63–4
visual imagery 38–9

waged labour, see employment
Wall Street Crash 20
Walsh, C.E. 55
Ward, E. 105
Warren, A. 94
Weiner, M. 84
Weiqiang, L. 95

Welsh, S. 105
white superiority 30
Wilson, C. 9, 56, 106
Wilson, K. 30
Woetzel, J. 63
women
feminisms 43, 46–9, 57, 58
work 62–4
Worboys, M. 68
work, see employment
World Bank 7, 13, 20, 23, 32, 36, 62,
69–70
'Education for the Knowledge
Economy' 73
World Development Indicators
34
World Conference Against Racism
109–10
World Health Organization (WHO)
68–9, 71

Xi Jinping 23

Yang, W.K. 57, 107, 108
Yanner, M. 105

Zapatistas 96, 111, 112
Zarakol, A. 41

Titles in the **Elgar Advanced Introductions** series include:

International Political Economy
Benjamin J. Cohen

The Austrian School of Economics
Randall G. Holcombe

Cultural Economics
Ruth Towse

Law and Development
Michael J. Trebilcock and Mariana Mota Prado

International Humanitarian Law
Robert Kolb

International Trade Law
Michael J. Trebilcock

Post Keynesian Economics
J.E. King

International Intellectual Property
Susy Frankel and Daniel J. Gervais

Public Management and Administration
Christopher Pollitt

Organised Crime
Leslie Holmes

Nationalism
Liah Greenfeld

Social Policy
Daniel Béland and Rianne Mahon

Globalisation
Jonathan Michie

Entrepreneurial Finance
Hans Landström

International Conflict and Security Law
Nigel D. White

Comparative Constitutional Law
Mark Tushnet

International Human Rights Law
Dinah L. Shelton

Entrepreneurship
Robert D. Hisrich

International Tax Law
Reuven S. Avi-Yonah

Public Policy
B. Guy Peters

The Law of International Organizations
Jan Klabbers

International Environmental Law
Ellen Hey

International Sales Law
Clayton P. Gillette

Corporate Venturing
Robert D. Hisrich

Public Choice
Randall G. Holcombe

Private Law
Jan M. Smits

Consumer Behavior Analysis
Gordon Foxall

Behavioral Economics
John F. Tomer

Cost-Benefit Analysis
Robert J. Brent

Environmental Impact Assessment
Angus Morrison Saunders

Comparative Constitutional Law
Second Edition
Mark Tushnet

National Innovation Systems
Cristina Chaminade, Bengt-Åke Lundvall and Shagufta Haneef

Ecological Economics
Matthias Ruth

Private International Law and Procedure
Peter Hay

Freedom of Expression
Mark Tushnet

Law and Globalisation
Jaakko Husa

Regional Innovation Systems
Bjørn T. Asheim, Arne Isaksen and Michaela Trippl

International Political Economy
Second Edition
Benjamin J. Cohen

International Tax Law
Second Edition
Reuven S. Avi-Yonah

Social Innovation
Frank Moulaert and Diana MacCallum

The Creative City
Charles Landry

International Trade Law
Michael J. Trebilcock and Joel Trachtman

European Union Law
Jacques Ziller

Planning Theory
Robert A. Beauregard

Tourism Destination Management
Chris Ryan

International Investment Law
August Reinisch

Sustainable Tourism
David Weaver

Austrian School of Economics
Second Edition
Randall G. Holcombe

U.S. Criminal Procedure
Christopher Slobogin

Platform Economics
Robin Mansell and W. Edward Steinmueller

Public Finance
Vito Tanzi

Feminist Economics
Joyce P. Jacobsen

Human Dignity and Law
James R. May and Erin Daly

Space Law
Frans G. von der Dunk

National Accounting
John M. Hartwick

Legal Research Methods
Ernst Hirsch Ballin

Privacy Law
Megan Richardson

International Human Rights Law
Second Edition
Dinah L. Shelton

Law and Artificial Intelligence
*Woodrow Barfield and
Ugo Pagello*

Politics of International
Human Rights
David P. Forsythe

Community-based Conservation
Fikret Berkes

Global Production Networks
Neil M. Coe

Mental Health Law
Michael L. Perlin

Law and Literature
Peter Goodrich

Creative Industries
John Hartley

Global Administration Law
Sabino Cassese

Housing Studies
William A.V. Clark

Global Sports Law
Stephen F. Ross

Public Policy
B. Guy Peters

Empirical Legal Research
Herbert M. Kritzer

Cities
Peter J. Taylor

Law and Entrepreneurship
Shubha Ghosh

Mobilities
Mimi Sheller

Technology Policy
*Albert N. Link and James A.
Cunningham*

Urban Transport Planning
Kevin J. Krizek and David A. King

Legal Reasoning
*Larry Alexander and Emily
Sherwin*

Sustainable Competitive
Advantage in Sales
Lawrence B. Chonko

Law and Development
Second Edition
*Mariana Mota Prado and Michael
J. Trebilcock*

Law and Renewable Energy
Joel B. Eisen

Experience Economy
Jon Sundbo

Marxism and Human Geography
Kevin R. Cox

Maritime Law
Paul Todd

American Foreign Policy
Loch K. Johnson

Water Politics
Ken Conca

Business Ethics
John Hooker

Employee Engagement
Alan M. Saks and Jamie A. Gruman

Governance
Jon Pierre and B. Guy Peters

Demography
Wolfgang Lutz

Environmental Compliance and Enforcement
LeRoy C. Paddock

Migration Studies
Ronald Skeldon

Landmark Criminal Cases
George P. Fletcher

Comparative Legal Methods
Pier Giuseppe Monateri

U.S. Environmental Law
E. Donald Elliott and Daniel C. Esty

Gentrification
Chris Hamnett

Family Policy
Chiara Saraceno

Law and Psychology
Tom R. Tyler

Advertising
Patrick De Pelsmacker

New Institutional Economics
Claude Ménard and Mary M. Shirley

The Sociology of Sport
Eric Anderson and Rory Magrath

The Sociology of Peace Processes
John D. Brewer

Social Protection
James Midgley

Corporate Finance
James A. Brickley and Clifford W. Smith Jr

U.S. Federal Securities Law
Thomas Lee Hazen

Cybersecurity Law
David P. Fidler

The Sociology of Work
Amy S. Wharton

Marketing Strategy
George S. Day

Scenario Planning
Paul Schoemaker

Financial Inclusion
Robert Lensink, Calumn Hamilton and Charles Adjasi

Children's Rights
Gamze Erdem Türkelli and Wouter Vandenhole

Sustainable Careers
Jeffrey H. Greenhaus and Gerard A. Callanan

Business and Human Rights
Peter T. Muchlinski

Spatial Statistics
Daniel A. Griffith and Bin Li

The Sociology of the Self
Shanyang Zhao

Artificial Intelligence in Healthcare
Thomas H. Davenport, John Glaser and Elizabeth Gardner

Central Banks and Monetary Policy
Jakob de Haan and Christiaan Pattipeilohy

Megaprojects
Nathalie Drouin and Rodney Turner

Social Capital
Karen S. Cook

Elections and Voting
Ian McAllister

Negotiation
Leigh Thompson and Cynthia S. Wang

Youth Studies
Howard Williamson and James E. Côté

Private Equity
Paul A. Gompers and Steven N. Kaplan

Digital Marketing
Utpal Dholakia

Water Economics and Policy
Ariel Dinar

Disaster Risk Reduction
Douglas Paton

Social Movements and Political Protests
Karl-Dieter Opp

Radical Innovation
Joe Tidd

Pricing Strategy and Analytics
Vithala R. Rao

Bounded Rationality
Clement A. Tisdell

International Food Law
Neal D. Fortin

International Conflict and Security Law
Second Edition
Nigel D. White

Entrepreneurial Finance
Second Edition
Hans Landström

US Civil Liberties
Susan N. Herman

Resilience
Fikret Berkes

Insurance Law
Robert H. Jerry, III

Law and Religion
Frank S. Ravitch

Social Policy
Second Edition
Daniel Béland and Rianne Mahon

Substantive Criminal Law
Stephen J. Morse

Cross-Border Insolvency Law
Reinhard Bork

Critical Global Development
Uma Kothari and Elise Klein